491.59 ABID
Abid, Zain-ul-Abdin Khan.
Pushtu made easy =Pushtu rozmarra,
or, Every day Pushtu /

PUSHTU MADE EASY
PUSHTU ROZMARA
OR
"EVERY- DAY PUSHTU"

PUSHTU MADE EASY
PUSHTU ROZMARA
OR
"EVERY- DAY PUSHTU"

PART - I
PUSHTU GRAMMAR

PART - II
COLLOQUIAL
Various Useful Terms

PART - III
ENGLISH AND PUSHTU VOCABULARY

AIN-UL-ABDIN KHAN-ABID

ASIAN EDUCATIONAL SERVICES
NEW DELHI ★ MADRAS ★ 2008

ASIAN EDUCATIONAL SERVICES

* 6A SHAHPUR JAT, NEW DELHI - 110 049
   Tel. : +91-11- 26491586, 26494059 Fax : 011- 26494946
   email : aes@aes.ind.in

* 2/15, 2nd FLOOR, ANSARI ROAD,
   DARYAGANJ, NEW DELHI - 1100 02
   Tel : +91- 11- 23262044
   email : aesdg@aes.ind.in

* 19, (NEW NO. 40), BALAJI NAGAR FIRST STREET,
   ROYAPETTAH, CHENNAI - 600 014
   Tel. : +91- 44 - 28133040 / 28131391 Fax : 044 - 28131391
   email : asianeds@md3.vsnl.net.in

www.aes.ind.in

Printed and Hand-Bound in India

First Published : Nowshera, 1917
First AES Reprint : New Delhi, 2001
Third AES Reprint : New Delhi, 2008

ISBN: 8120615948
EAN : 9788120615946

Published by Gautam Jetley
For ASIAN EDUCATIONAL SERVICES
6A, Shahpur Jat, New Delhi - 110 049.
Processed by AES Publications Pvt. Ltd., New Delhi-110049
Printed at Jaico Printers, Darya Ganj, New Delhi - 110 002

PREFACE.

While studying with Military officers and others for the Elementary Examination in Pashto, I have often been asked by them to procure some kind of text book, which might enable them to work at the language by themselves. The absence of an official text book for the Examination, and the difficulty of giving tuition to candidates without such a book, have led me to compile this work in the sure belief that it will prove a real help in passing the examination.

I am aware that many Vocabularies, Guides, Grammars, etc. exist which have been compiled by various Munshis who have very little knowledge of the Pathan's language, as few of them, if any, are Yusufzá-is by birth. I have the advantage of being a Pathan by birth and have spent all my life in districts inhabited by Pathans.

I am therefore thoroughly qualified to give correct information as to the various local dialects which prove a stumbling block to candidates, concerning which most munshis lack intimate knowledge. Their works show many faults, chief amongst which is the use of a Hindustani word or phrase where an idiomatic Pashto equivalent exists.

ABBREVIATIONS.

N.	=	Nominative.	n. s.	=	Noun singular.
Ag.	=	Agent.	n. p.	=	Noun plural.
G.	=	Genitive.	M. s.	=	Masculine singular.
D.	=	Dative.	M. p.	=	Masculine plural.
Ac.	=	Accusative.	F. s.	=	Feminine singular.
Ab.	=	Ablative.	F. p	=	Feminine plural.
Loc.	=	Locative.	Adj.	=	Adjective.
V.	=	Vocative.	Adv.	=	Adverb.
Prep.	=	Preposition.	Pron.	=	Pronoun.
V. t.	=	Verb transitive.	R.	=	Root.
V. int.	=	Verb intransitive.	P.	=	Past participle.

PRONOUNCIATION.

ai	is	pronounced	"ay"	as in	way.
á-i	„		"i-ee"	as diphthong i-e in	ti-e.
h (accented)	„		"uh"	"u" must precede this	"h".
h (unaccented)	„		"ah"	"a" must precede this	"h".
i (final)	„		"ee"	as in	free.
i (medial)	„		"i"	„	kit.
ú (accented)	„		"oo"	„	coóper.
u (unaccented)	„		"o"	„	go
áu	is	„	"a-ow"	„	plough.
á	„	„	"a" long	„	fär.
a	„	„	"a" short	„	fat.
d	„	„	"d" hard	„	add.
r	„	„	"r" „	„	purr.
t	„	„	"t" „	„	butt.
ch	„	„	"ch" in one	„	church.
zh	„	„	"zh" „	„	measure.
gh	„	„	"gh" guttural	„	Afghán.
kh	„	„	"kh" „	„	Loch.

Part I.

GRAMMAR.

ARTICLES.

(*a*) In Pashto there is no article to correspond with the English articles " a " " an " and " the " thus:—

Khán may mean a chief or the chief.

Lakhkar may mean an army or the army.

(*b*) The numeral "yau" (one), is however, employed for the indefinite articles "a" or "an" when the object requires to be specially mentioned as :—

Yau spáhi, means a soldier or a certain soldier.

Yau afsar, means an officer or a certain officer.

(*c*) The Demonstrative Pronouns "Dá" or "Daghah" (this), and "Haghah" (that) are used for the definite article "the" as :—

Dá or Daghah topak, means this or the rifle,

Haghah túrah, means that or the sword.

NOUNS.

Nouns in Pashto have only two genders, and two numbers, i. e. Masculine and Feminine, and Singular and Plural.

GENDERS.

Masculine, Nominative Singular.

No.	Masculine.		Feminine.
	EXAMPLES.		EXCEPTIONS
1	Nouns ending in "ai"	Sarai a man.	
2	Nouns ending in final accented "h"	Márghuh a bird.	Cháruh=a big knife, Obuh=water, Kholuh= the mouth, Tiáruh=darkness, Khorzuh= a neice, Tarluh=cousin (fem), Linduh=a bow.
3	Nouns ending in "i" if denoting profession.	Khkári a hunter.	
4	(a) Nouns ending in a consonant, (b) including long "áu", (c) and accented "ú"	(a) Malak, a head man.	*Paltan=a regiment, Lár=a road, Miásht=a month, Wraz=a day, Kúzhdan=betrothal, Brastan=a quilt, Laman=a skirt, Mechan= a hand mill, Dúrshal=a door frame, Mangul= the paw, Sangul=the elbow, Sarman=a skin, Maraz=a quail, Stan=a needle, Smas=a cave, Waryaz=cloud, Gamanz=a comb, Ghojal= a cowshed.
		(b) Paráu Camp.	
		(c Dárú a medicine or powder.	Járí=a Broom.

* These are real feminine nouns ending in unaccented " ah " but their final " h " is euphonically rejected. They sometimes take " ah " as Paltanah=a regiment.

The Genders of some nouns are easily distinguished by their meanings such as :—

MASCULINE.

Zoe = a son. Hati = an elephant. Toti = a parrot.

FEMININE.

Mor = mother. Tandár = uncle's wife. Ngor = son's wife.
Lúr = daughter. Dái = a nurse. Ndror = husband's sister.
Tror = aunt. Merman = a mistress. Yor = husband's
Khor = sister. Ba-an = a rival wife. brother's wife.
Wrandár = brother's wife.

FEMININE.
Nominative Singular.

No.	Feminine.		EXCEPTIONS — Masculine.
1	Nouns ending in " á-i "	Jiná-i, a girl.	Pá-i = milk (pl).
2	Nouns ending in final unaccented " h "	Khazah, a woman.	
3	Nouns ending in "i" if denoting condition.	Badi, an evil.	Wakhti = early, Khúi = habit, Sabá-i = morning, Tari = sugar etc.
4	All nouns ending in (a) "á" (b) "e" and (c) unaccented "u" or "o"	a) Ghwá, a cow. b) *Cháe, Tea. c) Shádo, a monkey.	Jolá = a weaver, Begá = evening or last night or to-night, Sabá = to-morrow, Káká = uncle (p), Mámá = uncle (m), Ashná = a friend, Sandá = a buffalo (bull), and all others of the foreign derivative ending in "á". Zoe = son, Mra-e = slave.

* Most of those nouns ending in " e " whose singular end in " h " are of the feminine gender and plural numbers as:—weenah (sing.) = blood; weene (plu.) = bloods.

FORMATION OF GENDERS.
The Feminine is formed from the masculine by the following rules:—

No.	How formed.		Masculine.	Feminine.
1	Masculine nouns ending in "ai" change "ai" into:—	"á-i"	Spai = a dog.	Spá-i = a bitch.
2	Masculine nouns ending in "ah" change "ah" into:—	"anah"	Melmah = a guest.	Melmanah = a guest.
3	Masculine nouns ending in "i" change "i" into:—	"á-i" or "anrah"	Dobi = a washerman.	Dobá-i or Dobaurah = a washer woman.
4	Masculine nouns ending in a †consonant form their feminine by merely adding to the last letter:—	"ah"	Malak = a head man.	Malakah = a head woman.

†Those masculine nouns ending in a consonant having "ú" in the last syllable change "ú" into short "a" before adding "ah" for feminine as :—pukhtún = a pathan man, pukhtanah = a pathan woman.

EXCEPTIONS.

The following nouns show their genders by their meanings, and are exceptions to the above rules:—

MASCULINE.			FEMININE.		
Nikuh	=	grand father.	Niyá	=	grand mother.
Plár	=	father.	Mor	=	mother.
Plandar	=	Step father.	Merah	=	step mother.
Skhar	=	father in law.	Khwákhe	=	mother in law.
Awkhe	=	brother in law.	Khine	=	sister in law.
Truh	=	uncle (paternal)	Tror	=	aunt (paternal)
Tarbúr	=	cousin.	Tarluh	=	cousin.
Sakhtan	=	husband.	Khazah	=	wife.
Wror	=	brother.	Khor	=	sister.
Zoe	=	son.	Lúr	=	daughter.
Zalmai	=	youth.	Peghlah	=	a maid.
Sarai	=	a man.	Khazah	=	a woman.
Halak	=	a boy.	Jiná-i	=	a girl.
Kháwand	=	master.	Merman	=	mistress.
Khorae	=	nephew sister's.	Khorzuh	=	niece.
Mrae	=	a slave.	Winzah	=	a slave.
As	=	a horse.	Aspah	=	mare.

Derivative masculine nouns ending in "á" form their feminine by adding "gá-i" as:—jola = a weaver, jola gá-i = weaver's wife.

Cháchá = uncle (paternal), cháchi = aunt (paternal) and Mámá = uncle (maternal), mámi = aunt (maternal), are the common exceptions.

NUMBERS.
To form nominative plural from nominative singular.
MASCULINE.

No.	Rule.		Examples.		Exceptions.
			Singular.	Plural.	
1	All masculine nouns which do not come under the following rules generally add :—	If animate "án" if inanimate "únah"	Spáhi, soldier. Fouz, army.	Spáhi-án, soldiers. Fouzúnah, armies.	
2	Masculine nouns ending in "ai" change "ai" into : —	"i"	Sarai, man.	Sari, men.	Monrgai=boat man, Monrgán=boat men, Kúhai=water well, Kúhian=water wells etc.
3	Masculine nouns ending in "ún"; and a few of the masculine ending in "ah" (if a human being) change their final "ún" or "ah" into:—	"ánuh"	Pukhtún, pathan. Melmah, guest.	Pukhtánuh, pathans Melmánuh, guests,	
4	Masculine nouns ending in "á" and "ú" accented add :—	"gán"	Sandá, buffalo(m) Melú, Bear,	Sandágán, buffaloes (m) Melúgan, Bears.	Ashná=friend, Ashnáyán=friends, Múlá=priest, Múlayán=priests, Kandú=corn bin, Kandúwán=corn bins.
5	Masculine nouns of one syllable add :—	"uh"	Ghal, thief.	Ghaluh, thieves.	Khar=an ass, Kharuh or Khrúnah=asses etc.
6	Masculine nouns indicating sounds add :—	"hár"	Krap, Bang.	Kraphár, Bangs.	

FEMININE.

No.	Rule.		Examples.		Exceptions.
			Singular.	Plural.	
1	All feminine nouns which do not come under the following rules generally add:—	"e"	Paltan, Regiment	Paltane, Regiments.	
2	Feminine nouns ending in "á-i" generally undergo no change, but sometimes change "á-i" into:—	"yáne"	Berá-i, Boat.	Beryáne, Boats.	
3	* Feminine nouns ending in "i" change "i" into:—	"á-í"	Neki, virtue.	Neká-í, virtues.	
4	Feminine nouns ending in "á", and "u" or "o" (unaccented) add:—	"gáne"	Ghwá, Cow. Pisho, cat.	Ghwágáne, Cows. Pishogáne, cats.	

* Feminine nouns ending in "i" sometimes change this "i" into "yáne" as :—neki=virtue, nekyáne = virtues ; cháchi = aunt (paternal), cháchyáne = aunts.

Note—Those masculine and feminine nouns having "uh" and "ah" in the final, drop these finals before adding "e" for plural as :—Khazah = woman, Khaze = women.

The Plural of the following masculine and feminine nouns are formed irregularly :—

SINGULAR.		PLURAL.	
Nikuh	= grand father.	Nikúnah or Nikán	=grand fathers.
Plár	= father.	Plarúnah or Pláran	=fathers.
Mor	= mother.	Mende or Moryáne	=mothers.
Wror	= brother.	Wrúnrah	=brothers.
Khor	= sister.	Khwende	=sisters.
Truh	= uncle (paternal)	Trúnah	=uncles.
Tror	= aunt (paternal).	Troráne	=aunts.
Mámi	= aunt (maternal).	Mámiyáne or Mámigáne	=aunts.
Zoe	= son.	Záman	=sons.
Lúr	= daughter.	Lúnrah	=daughters.
Wráruh	= nephew, brother's.	Wrerúnah	=nephews.
Jiná-i	= a girl.	Jinaká-i	=girls.
Sakhtan or Meruh	= husband.	Sakhtanúnah or Marúnah	=husbands.
Skhar	=father in law.	Skharúnah or Skharán	=fathers in law.
Khwákhe	=mother in law.	Khwákheyáne or Khwakhegane	=mothers in law.
Khine	=sister in law.	Khine or Khinyáne	=sisters in law.
Ngor	=son's wife.	Ngende	=son's wives.
Jewar	=husband's brother.	Lewrúnah	=husband's brothers.
Ndror	=husband's sister.	Ndroráne or Ndroryáne	=husband's sisters.
Yor	=husband's brother's wife.	Yúnrah	=husband's brother's wives.
As	=a horse.	Asúnah	=horses.

DIMINUTIVE NOUNS.

As a general rule they are formed by adding "Gai" for masculine, and "Gá-i" for feminine to the simple nouns, as :—

Bár = a load, Bárgai = a small load.
Khrab = a she donkey, Khrgá-i = a small she donkey.

NOTE—Some nouns take the addition of the following endings to form the diminutives :—

No.	Endings.		Examples.			
	Masculine.	Feminine.	Simple nouns.		Diminutive nouns.	
			Masculine.	Feminine.	Masculine.	Feminine.
1	"Gútai"	"Gútá-i" or "Gúte"	Charg, a cock.	Chargah, a hen.	Chargútai, a chick.	Chargútá-i, a chick.
2	"ai"	"á-i"	Márghuh, a cock bird.	Márghuh, a hen bird.	Marghai=a little bird.	Marghá.i=a little bird.
3	"Kai" or "úkai"	"Ká-i" or "úká.i"	Loar, a sickle.	Cháruh, a knife.	Loarúkai=a small sickle	Charúká-i, a small knife
4	"Rai" or "úrai"	"Rá-i" or "úrá.i" or "úre"	Mangak or Mng=a rat.	Mangakah or Magah, a rat.	Mangakúrai a mouse.	Mangakúre a mouse.

ABSTRACT NOUNS.

These are generally formed by adding "tob" and "wále" for masculine, and "wali" for feminine, to the simple nouns and adjectives as :—

Spáhi = a soldier, Spáhitob = soldiering.
Kog = crooked, Kogwále = crookedness.
Khpal = a relative, Khpalwáli = relationship.

NOTE—The abstract nouns of some simple nouns and adjectives are formed by adding the following endings to them :—

No.	Endings.	Simple nouns and adjectives.	Abstract nouns.	No.	Endings	Simple nouns and adjectives.	Abstract nouns.
1	"Tiá"	Nájorah, sick.	Nájortiá, illness.	5	"Gali"	Rikhtine, truthful.	Rikhtingali, truthfulness.
2	"Tún"	Kundah=a widow.	Kundtún, widowhood.	6	"Akht"	Jor=well, agree.	Jorakht, agreeable.
3	"Edan"	Rogh=well, healthy.	Roghedan, healthiness.	7	"i"	Ashná=a friend.	Ashná-i, friendship.
4	"ún"	Zhwand=life	Zhwandún, liveliness.	8	"á"	Ghal=a thief.	Ghlá=theft.

NOTE—The final "ai" "uh", "áh", "i" and "e" of some nouns and adjectives are dropped before adding the above endings, in forming the diminutive, and abstract nouns.

PREPOSITIONS.

Precede the noun.	Follow the noun.	Noun to be placed between the hyphen.
Da = of	tah ⎫ lah ⎪ larah ⎬ = to wartah ⎪ warlarah ⎭ daparah = for. dapasah = above. Sarah = with, along. Sakhah = near, in possession of.	Da —pah meanz ke = in the midst of. Pah—ke = in. Pah—bánde = on. Tre—pore = upto. Lah—nah ⎫ Da —nah ⎬ = from Da —lánde = under.

Note—The first or the second half part of the double preposition is sometimes omitted.

DECLENSION.

OBLIQUE CASES.

All kinds of nouns of both genders and numbers when governed by a preposition are inflected, or in other words are put in the oblique cases.

OBLIQUE SINGULAR.

Masculine nouns ending in " ai ", and feminine nouns ending in " ah ", or " uh ", or ending in a consonant, are declinable both in the singular and plural. All others are declinable only in the plural.

Those nouns which are declinable in the singular, both masculine and feminine, form their singular oblique from their nominative plural, that is to say the oblique singular and nominative plural are the same as :—

Sarai = a man, Sari = men or by a man; and by changing " ah " or " uh " of the feminine nouns into " e " as :—Khazah = a woman, Khaze = women or by a woman as :—Paltan = a regiment, Paltane = regiments or by a regiment.

OBLIQUE PLURAL.

The oblique plural is formed by adding " o " to the nominative plural of all kinds of *nouns both masculine and feminine.

* Those masculine and feminine nouns whose nominative plural end in "i", "ah", or "uh", "á-i" and "e", drop these finals before adding "o" to form the oblique plural.

Declension of all kinds of nouns declinable

OBLIQUE SINGULAR.

Case.	Masculine.				Feminine.			
N.	Sarai. a man.	Márghuh, a bird.	Khkári, a hunter.	Malak, a headman	Khazah, a woman.	Silá-i, a storm.	Ghwá, a cow.	Paltan, a regiment.
G.	da sari, of a man.	da márghuh, of a bird.	da khkári, of a hunter.	da malak, of a headman	da khaze, of a woman.	da silá-i, of a storm.	da ghwá, of a cow.	da paltane, of a regiment.
D.	Sari tah, to a man.	Márghuh tah, to a bird.	Khkári tah, to a hunter.	Malak tah, to a headman	Khaze tah, to a woman.	Silái tah, to a storm.	Ghwá tah, to a cow.	Paltane tah to a regiment.
Ac.	Sarai, a man.	Márghuh a bird.	Khkári, a hunter.	Malak, a headman	Khazah, a woman.	Silá-i, a storm.	Ghwá, a cow.	Paltan, a regiment.
Loc.	Pah sari bánde, on a man.	Pah márghuh bánde, on a bird.	Pah khkári bánde, on a hunter.	Pah malak bánde, on a headman	Pah khaze bánde, on a woman.	Pah silái bánde, on a storm.	Pah ghwá bánde, on a cow.	Pah paltane bánde, on a regiment.
Ab.	Lah sari nah, from a man.	Lah márghuh nah, from a bird	Lah khkari nah, from a hunter.	Lah malak nah, from a headman	Lah khaze nah, from a woman.	Lah silái nah, from a storm.	Lah ghwá nah, from a cow.	Lah paltane nah from a regiment.
V.	ai sariah, oh man.	ai márghuh, oh bird.	ai khkári, oh hunter.	ai malakah oh headman	ai khaze, oh woman.	ai silá-i, oh storm.	ai ghwá, oh cow.	ai paltane, oh regiment.
Ag.	Sari, by a man.	Márghuh, by a bird.	Khkári by a hunter.	Malak, by a headman	Khaze, by a woman.	Silá-i, by a storm.	Ghwa, by a cow.	Paltane, by a regiment.

Note 1—' áno", "gáno" and "úno" are sometimes shortened to "o" or "go" in the

Note 2—All masculine nouns except those ending in "uh" or "ah", "á" and "ú" Sáhib=master, sáhibah=oh master.

Note 3—"nah" the second part of the preposition "lah-nah" (from) is often dropped or Lah daftarah (from the office).

and indeclinable, both masculine and feminine.

OBLIQUE PLURAL.

Masculine.				Feminine.			
Sari, men	Márghán, birds.	Khkárián, hunters.	Malakán, headmen.	Khaze, women.	Silá i, storms.	Ghwágáne cows.	Paltane, regiments.
da saro, of men.	da márgháno, of birds.	da khkáriáno of hunters.	da malakáno, of headmen.	da khazo, of women.	da silo, of storms.	da ghwágáno of cows.	da paltano, of regiments.
Saro tah, to men.	Márghán tah, to birds.	Khkáriáno tah, to hunters.	Malakáno tah, to headmen.	Khazo tah, to women.	Silo tah, to storms.	Ghwágáno tah, to cows.	Paltano tah to regiments.
Sari, men.	Márghán birds.	Khkárián, hunters.	Malakán, headmen.	Khaze, women.	Sila-i, storms.	Ghwágáne cows.	Paltane, regiments.
Pah saro bánde, on men.	Pah márgháno bánde, on birds.	Pah khkáriáno bánde, on hunters.	Pah malakáno bánde, on headmen.	Pah khazo bánde, on women.	Pah silo bánde, on storms.	Pah ghwágáno bánde, on cows.	Pah paltano bánde, on regiments.
Lah saro nah, from men.	Lah márgháno nah, from birds	Lah khkariáno nah, from hunters.	Lah malakáno nah, from headmen.	Lah khazo nah, from women.	Lah silo nah, from storms.	Lah ghwágáno nah, from cows.	Lah paltano nah from regiments.
ai saro, oh men.	ai márgháno, oh birds.	ai khkáriáno oh hunters.	ai malakáno, oh headmen.	ai khazo, oh women.	ai silo, oh storms.	ai ghwágáno oh cows.	ai paltano, oh regiments.
Saro, by men.	Márgháno, by birds.	Khkáriáno, by hunters.	Malakáno, by headmen	Khazo, by women.	Silo, by storms.	Ghwágáno by cows.	Paltano, by regiments.

oblique cases of plural as :—goragáno shortened to "garáo"=by British soldiers.

(accented), take the addition of "ah" to the oblique singular in the vocative case as :—

and "ah" is added to the oblique singular in the ablative case as :—Lah daftar nah

ADJECTIVES.

Adjectives are always placed before their nouns and agree in gender, number, and case with the nouns they qualify as :— Khuh nokar = a good servant.

NOTE—An adjective is put in after its noun when used as a noun as :—Sarai khuh dai=the man is good.

All adjectives ending in a consonant are of the masculine gender; their plural and declension are like those of the masculine nouns.

To form the feminine of adjectives.

No.	Rule.		Examples.		Exceptions.	
			Masculine	Feminine	Masculine	Feminine.
1	Adjective ending in a consonant add :—	" ah "	Dang, tall.	Dangah, tall.	Drúnd, heavy.	Dranah, heavy.
2	Adjective ending in "ai" change "ai" into :—	" á-i "	Garandai, swift.	Garandá-i, swift.	Tagai, thirsty. Wogai, hungry. Starai, tired. Kamzorai weak.	Tage, thirsty. Woge, hungry. Stare, tired. Kamzore, weak.
3	Adjective ending in a vowel and "h" remains unchanged:—	un- changed	Bekhe, useless. Khuh, good.	Bekhe, useless. Khuh, good.	Loe, big.	Loeah, big.

NOTE 1—Adjectives ending in a consonant add "e" for feminine plural as :— Tor=black, Tore=(feminine plural) ; those adjectives ending in "ai" and ' h" drop these before adding "e" for feminine plural as :—Khuh=good, khe=good (feminine plural).

NOTE 2—Adjectives having "i" and "u" or "o" in their syllables change "i" and "u" into short "a" when forming feminine singular as :—Súr=red, sarah=(feminine) ahin=green, shanah=(feminine).

The exceptions to the foot note No. 2 are.

Masculine.	Feminine.	Masculine.	Feminine.
Tor=black.	Torah.	Sor=mounted.	Swarah.
Tod=warm.	Taudah.	Khor=scattered.	Khwarah.
Khog=sweet.	Khwagah.	Lúnd=wet.	Laundah.
Gud=lame.	Gudah.	Loe=big.	Loeah.

COMPARISON.

The comparative is formed by placing the compared noun in the ablative case, i. e., between the preposition "lah—nah" (from) and the adjective after it, agreeing in gender, number, and case with its noun as :—

úkh lah hati nah garandai dai,
The camel is swifter than the elephant.

The superlative is formed by using "tol" (all) or "wárah" (whole) before the compared noun as :—

Haghah lah talo spáhiáno nah túrzan dai,
He is the bravest of all the soldiers.

Note—"Beshánah", "Behisábah", "Behaddah" (out of account or limit), "Hamah" "Jumlah" (all, lot), "Z yát" and "der" (very, more, much, many) etc. the nouns of multitude, are sometimes also placed before or after the compared object in the degree of superlative.

PRONOUNS.
PERSONAL.

Case.	Singular.			Plural.		
	1	2	3	1	2	3
N.	I=zuh.	Thou=tuh.	He, she, it and that, haghah.	* We, múng.	You, táso.	They, haghoe.
Ag.	By me=má	By thee=tá	By him or it, haghuh. By her, haghe.	Bv us, múng.	By you, táso.	By them, haghoe.
G.	My=zamá.	Thy=stá.	His, its, da haghuh. Her, da haghe.	Our, zamúng.	Your, stáso.	Their, da haghoe.
D.	To me, má tah.	To thee, tá tah.	To him, it, haghuh tah. To her, haghe tah.	To us, múng tah.	To you, táso tah.	To them, haghoe tah.
Ac.	I=zuh.	Thou=tuh.	He, she, it and that, haghah.	We, múng.	You, táso.	They, haghoe.
Ab.	From me, lah-má nah.	From thee, lah tá nah.	From him, it, that, lah haghuh nah. From her, lah haghe nah.	From us, lah múng nah	From you, lah táso nah.	From them, lah haghoe nah.
Loc.	On me, pa má bánde	On thee, pah tá bánde	On him, it, that, pah haghuh bánde. On her, pah haghe bánde.	On us, pah múng bánde.	On you, pah táso bánde.	On them, pah haghoe bánde.
V.	Oh I, ai zuh.	Oh thou, ai tuh.	Oh he, she, it ai haghah.	Oh we, ai múng.	Oh you, ai táso.	Oh they, ai haghoe.

NOTE—The pronouns "zuh" (I) becomes má (by me etc.); "tuh" (thou) "tá" (by thee etc.); and haghah (he, it, that) haghuh (by him, it, that etc.); and haghah (she) haghe (by her etc.), in the agent and all other cases, except in the nominative, accusative and vocative cases.

* "ah" is sometimes added to "múng" (we) for euphony in all cases as:—múng (we) or múng ah.

THE SHORT POSSESSIVE PRONOUNS.

Person.	Sigular.	Plural.
1	Me = by me or my.	Mu = by us or ours.
2	De = by thee or thy.	Mu = by you or yours.
3	Ye = by him, her, it, that, or his, her its.	Ye = by them or their.

They are most commonly used in the place of the **Personal** Pronouns of the agent and Genitive cases, especially **when no** special emphasis is laid on the Personal Pronouns.

Note—The Personal Pronouns precede, while the Possessive Pronouns follow their nouns i. e. "zamá as or as, me" = my horse.

THE DATIVE PARTICLES.

Person.	Particle.	Singular and Plural.
1	Ra	= towards me, or us, or this side.
2	Dar	= towards thee, or you, or to thy, or your side.
3	War	= towards him, her, it, that, or them, or that side.

They are often joined to the preposition tah, lah, larah (to) the signs of the Dative case, and are also prefixed to verbs and adverbs to point out the person or place as :—Rá tah = to me, or to us; Tlal = to go, Dar tlal = (to come to thee, or you, or to thy, or your side); Bánde = on, upon, War bánde = on him, her, it, that.

DEMONSTRATIVE PRONOUNS.

Proximate.	Dá or *Daghah = this or these.	These are only used for the third Person Pronouns both Singular and Plural, masculine and feminine and declined like a feminine noun ending in "ah".
Remote.	Haghah = that or those.	

* "Dá" (this or these) is the shortened form of 'Daghah''; and "Dey" (this or he) is the idiomatical form of "Dá" or "Daghah" (this or these). "Dey" remains uninflected and "Dá" and "Haghah" are subject to inflection in the Oblique cases.

DECLENSION.

Case	SINGULAR. Masculine and Feminine.	PLURAL. Masculine and Feminine.
N.	Dá, or daghah = this. Haghah = that.	Dá, or daghah = these. Haghah = those.
Ag.	*De, or daghe, or duh = by this. Haghuh = by him or Haghe = by her or him.	De, or deo, or do, Daghe, or dui, or dagho, } by these. Haghe, or hagho, or hagheo, or haghúi, } by (those), them.
D.	De, or daghe tah = to this. †Duh, or daghuh, tah = to him. Haghe tah = to her or him.	De, or deo, or daghe, or dui, or dagho tah } to these. Haghe, or hagheo, Hagho, or haghúi tah } to (those), them.

* The inflected forms "de", "daghe", and "haghe" require their subjects to be mentioned after them.

† The forms "duh", or daghuh", and "haghe" apply to 3rd Person Singular masculine only.

Note—For 3rd Person Singular masculine and feminine, the final "á" of "dá" and "ah" of daghah and haghah are changed into "e", but the change of "á" or "ah" into (accented) "uh" is only for masculine in the oblique cases of singular; and for 3rd Person Plural masculine and feminine the final "á" of "dá" and "ah" of "daghah" and "haghah" are changed into "e" or "o"; and sometimes into "úi" or "eo" in the oblique cases of the plural.

INTERROGATIVE PRONOUNS.

1	Sok = who.	Applies to persons only, and its inflected form "chá" does not change its gender and number.
2	Suh = what.	Generally applies to inanimate objects but adjectively applies to animate objects too. It does not change its gender, number and case.
3	Kum = which	Applies to both animate and inanimate objects and is declined like an adjective ending in a consonant.
4	*So or somrah, how many, how much.	The former applies to both animate and inanimate objects and the latter applies to inanimate only. These both are indeclinable.

* "So" is the shortened form of "Somrah".

Inflection of Sok (who) and Kum (which).

Form.	Singular.		Plural.	
	Masculine.	Feminine.	Masculine.	Femiaine.
Nominative	Sok = who.	Sok = who.	Sok = who.	Sok = who.
Inflected.	Chá = by whom etc.	Chá = by whom etc.	Chá = by whom etc.	Chá = by whom etc.
Nominative	Kum = which	Kumah = which.	Kum = which	Kume = which
Inflected.	Kum = by which etc.	Kume = by which etc.	Kumo = by which etc.	Kumo = by which etc.

RELATIVE PRONOUNS.

| 1 | Chih = that. | It is unchangeable. |

NOTE—"Chih" ends a sentence and starts a fresh clause. It adds point to a speech. As a conjunction it has many significations such as "that", "when", "because", "as", "if", "whether", "while", and 'lest' etc. When it is combined with a correlative or interrogative pronoun it answers the interrogative as:—Kum sarai=which man, Kum chih nájorah dai=the one who is sick.

CORRELATIVE PRONOUNS.

EXAMPLES.

| 1 | Domrah, so much. | These are used in answering the interrogative pronoun "so" or "somrah" and undergo no change. | Somrah chih pakár di domrah yaosah. |
| 2 | Homrah, that much. | | Take away as much as is required. |

NOTE—'Domrah is the shortened form of Daghah Homrah (this much) and "Homrah" is the shortened form of "Haghah Homrah" (that much).

POSSESSIVE PRONOUNS.

There is no Possessive Pronoun is Pashto, they are supplied by the Reflexive Pronoun viz:—

| 1 | Khpal = own. | It is declined like an adjective ending in a consonant. |

Pakhpalah=means by one's self or one's own accord.

NOTE—When pakhpalah is joined to a noun it gives the idea of emphasis and speciality.

"Khpal" is used for all pronouns of the Genitive case, such as my, thy, his, her, our, your, and their, when a second pronoun is required to refer to the same person as the subject, as:—He went to his country = Haghah khpal mulk tah láruh.

NOTE—The short possessive pronouns are often employed for the possessive pronouns—vide page 15.

INDEFINITE PRONOUNS.

1	Sok = anyone, someone.	Applies to persons and its inflected form is chá.
2	Suh = some, something, anyone, anything	Generally refers to inanimate objects, sometimes to animate objects, and remains unchanged.
3	Zine or báze = some, certain.	Apply to both animate and inanimate objects and undergo no change except in the oblique plural where they take the addition of "o" after dropping their final "e"
4	Hes = anyone, anything.	Refers to both animate and inanimate objects and is always preceded by the negative "nah" or interrogative "sok" or a noun etc. in answering a question and is not subject to any inflection

NOTE—Some adjectives are commonly used as indefinite pronouns. They often join the interrogative or the indefinite pronouns or the indefinite numeral 'yau" to form the compound indefinite pronouns as :—

Adjective.	Compound indefinite pronouns.		Compound indefinite pronouns.	
	Masculine.	Feminine.	Masculine.	Feminine.
Bal = another.	Yau bal = another, one more. Bal yau = another one, one more.	Yawah balah. Balah yawah.	Bal sok = some one else, who else. Bal suh = something else, what else.	Balah sok. Balah suh.
Nor = others, more.	Nor sok = who else. Nor suh = what else.	Norah sok. Norah suh.	Nor so or nor somrah, how many, how much more. Nor der = many or much more.	Norah so or norah somrah Norah derah.
Har = every, each.	Har sok = every body. Har suh = everything, anything.	Harah sok. Harah suh.	Har yau = every one, each. Har so or har somrah, however many or much.	Harah yawah Harah so or harah somrah
Der = many, much.	Der sok = many or much others. Der suh = many or much else.	Derah sok. Derah suh.	Der nor = many or much more. Der der = many many or much much.	Derah norah. Derah derah.
Tol = all, whole.	Nor tol = all the remainder or the rest. Tol tál = in all.	Norah tolah. Tolah tálah.	Hes sok = nobody. Hes suh = nothing else, anything else. Suh nah suh = something or other.	Hes sok. Hes suh. Suh nah suh.

NEGATION AND PROHIBITION.

			EXAMPLES.
Negative.	Nah=no, not.	It is used with all kinds of tenses, except with the imperative of the second person singular and plural. In simple present tenses it generally precedes the verb and in compound tenses it is placed before the last auxiliary. Verbs which take the prefix of "wu" in the tenses, "nah" is placed after prefixing "wu". Verbs which do not admit the prefix of "wu", "nah" take between their two syllables.	Nah awri = he does not hear. Poh-e shawai nah dai = he has not understand. Haghah hes wu nah wayal = he said nothing. Zuh ken nah nástam = I did not sit.
Prohibitive.	Mah=dont, not.	It is only used with the Imperative of the second person singular and plural and is always placed before the verb. Verbs which take the prefix of "wu" for Imperative in the positive form, this "wu" must be rejected before prefixing "mah" in the prohibitive form.	Wu kah = do it. (sing.) Mah kawah = do not do it. Wu ká-i = do it. (plu.) Mah kawá-i = do not do it. (plu.)

AFFIRMITIVE.

	Ho=yes.	It remains unchanged.

ADVERBS.

Adverbs of place.	Adverbs of place.
Here = Daltah, dale, daghaltah.	Towards me, us, this = Rá hishtah.
There = Haltah, haghaltah.	Towards him, them, that. } = War hishtah.
Where = Chartah, kum záe.	
Outside = Bahar.	That way, that side. } Haghah khwá, haghah palau, haghah taraf.
Inside = Dananah.	To which direction = Pah kum lori.
Up = Portah, Pás.	At one side = Pah yawah dadah.
Down = Khkatah.	At this side = Pah de arkh.
Above = Dapásah.	Farthest, outward = Selmah.
Under = Lánde.	Everywhere, anywhere. { Har chartah, záe pah záe,
Far = Lare.	
Near = Nizde.	Nowhere = Hichartah.
In front = Wránde, Makh ke.	Somewhere or other. } = Chartah ná chartah
Behind = Wrusto.	On, upon = Bánde.
Backward, at back. } = Bertah, Pah shá.	Upside down = Lánde bánde.
Opposite = Makhah mukh.	Above it, upon it. } Pre dápásah, pre bánde
Round about = Cháperah.	Upper = Bar.
Neighbourhood = Khwá úshá.	Lower = Kúz.
Other side, (of the river etc. } = Pore.	All round about. { Gair cháperah, chár cháperah,
This side, (of the river etc.) } = Rá pore.	Right side = Khai taraf.
This way, this side. } = Hishta, de khwá, de palau.	Left hand = Kinr or gas lás.
	Close = Sakhah.

ADVERBS.

Adverbs of place.	Adverbs of time.
Close=Sakhah.	Early=Wakhti.
From afar=Lah wráyah, Lah lare.	Late=Náwakhtah.
Spot (the place of occurrence} =Mauqah.	Delay=Drang.
	Quickly=Zar Zar.
Degree, limit=Had.	Slowly=Wro wro.

ADVERBS OF TIME.	
Now=Aos.	At once, soon, immediately} =Samdasti, Pah you dam.
Again=Biyá	Instantly, without delay} =Sam dah lasáh.
Before=Pakhwá, wrúnbai, awal.	In the twinkling of an eye {=Da starge pah rap ke.
When=Kalah.	
After=Pas.	Continually, repeatedly} =Par lah pase.
Then=Halah.	Suddenly=Násápah.
Always= {Tal, Múdám, Har kalah, Hameshah.	Unexpectedly, unaware} =Nágúmánah.
Ever, (at any time)=Chare.	By chance=Nágahánah.
Never=Hechare, Hes kalah.	Presently, at the moment {=Filhálah, dá sáat, dá mál, dá wakhat.
Whenever = {Chare chih, Har kala chih.	
Since=Ráse.	In now a days {=Pah de shpo wrazo ke.
May hap, it behoves=Boyah.	Afterward, later on} =Pas tah, wrusto.
Perhaps, probably=gunde, Sháyad.	
Perhaps not=Dáse nah chih.	After this, in future {=Pas lah de, de nah pas, de pase.
At last=Akhir.	Up till now=Aosah pore.

ADVERBS.

Adverbs of time.	Adverbs of time.
Sometimes, now and then. = { Chare chare. / Kalah kalah.	Yesterday = Parún.
Occasionally = Kalah ná kalah.	Day before yesterday } = Bal parún, aormah wraz.
For ever = Tal tal or tal tre talah.	Second day before yesterday } = Lá bal parún, Lá aormah wraz
Frequently = Aksar.	Morning = Sahar.
Since when = Kalah ráse.	Evening = Mákhám.
Long since = { Larghúnai, / Pakhwá ráse.	Last night = Begá.
	Noon = Gharmah.
Time, turn = Wár, zal.	After noon or 2 p.m. = Máspakhin.
Once = Yau wár, yau zal.	4 p. m. = Mázigar.
In turn = Wár pah wár.	10 p. m, = Máskhotan.
How often = So wárah, so zalah.	Midnight = Nimah shpah.
Every time = Har wár, har zal.	Dead of night = Qlárah shúmah.
At this period = Pah de múdah.	2 a. m. = Peshmanai.
	4 a. m. = Charg báng.
In which season = Pah kúm mosam	This month = Da miásht.
To day = Nan,	Last month = { Terah miásht, / wrusto miásht.
Tomorrow = Sabá.	Next month = { Mukhke miásht, / balah miásht.
Day after tomorrow = Bal sabá.	
Second day after tomorrow } = Lá bal sabá.	This year = Sag kál.
To day & tomorrow = Nan aw sabá.	Last year = Parusah kál.

ADVERBS.

Adverbs of time.	Adverbs of quantity.
Next year = Bal kál, mukhke kál.	Who else=Nor sok.
Ancient time, } Pakhwáná-i old time. } zamánah.	What else=Nor suh.
	Another one=Bal yau.
Adverbs of quantity.	Every one=Har yau.
How much = So.	Nobody=Hes sok.
How many = Somrah.	Nothing=Hes nah.
So much, this much = Domrah.	Some one else=Bal sok.
That much= { Haghah homrah, homrah.	Something else=Bal suh.
	Whoever=Har sok.
Much, many = Der.	Whatever=Har suh.
More=Ziyát.	Some one or other, anyone } =Sok nah sok.
Less, short=Kam.	
A little=Lagkúti.	Something or other, anything. } =Suh nah suh.
Every=Har.	
About=Takhminan qariban.	In all=Tol tál.
However many, as many as. } =Har so.	Whole=Wár h.
	Both=Dwárah.
However much, as much as. } =Har somrah.	**Adverbs of similitude.**
Many or much more=Nor der.	
Even more=Lá ziyát.	Thus, like this=Dáse, daghah se.
It is enough, sufficient, that will do. } =Bas dai, káfi dai, der dai, bas kah.	Like that, such as that } =Hase, haghah se.
	As, like=Lakah.
Upto degree=Tre hadah pore.	Same as, likely. } =Ghunde.
Beyond limit or degree. } =Behddah, lah haddah ziyát.	Means, that is to say=Yáne.

ADVERBS.

Adverbs of similitude.	Adverbs of admonition.
For example==Misál, masalan.	Befitting, adviseable = { Khá-i báeduh di, munásib di.
In short=Landah.	
Proverb=Matal.	Dont do it again = { Biyá dáse mah kawah.
In this way, in this manner } =Dá shán, de ghunde.	**Common Pashto adverbs**
In that way, in that manner } =Haghah shán, haghah ghunde.	Why=Wale, suh lah.
Of this kind=Dá kisam.	Verily=Kho.
Of this sort or colour=Dá rang.	How=Sangah, suh rangah.
Of that kind=Haghah kisam.	Any how=Har rangah.
Of that sort or colour. } =Haghah rang.	Uselessly, for nothing = { Wuch pah wuchah, behisah.
	At all event=Khwá makhwá.
Adverbs of admonition.	Certainly, doubtless=Beshakah.
Mind, take care=Paham kawah.	What for = { Suh lah, suh daparah, wale.
Becareful=Khabar dár shah.	For this reason = { Lah de sababah, lah de wajeh, lah de jehatah, lah de nah.
Be cautious=Bedár shah.	
Know, mark=Poh-e shah.	
Remember=Yád larah.	For nothing=Hase.
Beware=Khabar shah.	At all=Hado, bekhi.
Look out=Wugorah.	Not at all=Lah sarah.
Be a man=Sarai shah.	At least=Kho.
Dont be a fool= { Kamaqal kegah mah.	Unless=So chih.
	Yes=Ho.
Be wise=Hukhiár shah.	No, not=Nah.
About (concern)=Pah bábat.	Dont=Mah.

Interjections.	Interjections
Oh=Ai, ao.	Get away=Pishe (applies to cats).
Alas, alas=Hái bái.	Get away = { Kare (applies to poultry) / shi (applies to birds). }
Oh my=Wá-i wá-i.	
Pity, sorrow, alas=Armán, afsos.	Death to him, it } =Mur shah, mirát shah.
Would to God=Káshki, dreghah.	Be ruined=Wrán shah.
Fie=Tobah.	Death to its owner = { Sukhtan or Lháwand / yi mur shah. }
Mercy, peace=Amán.	
Well done, bravo = { Sháh básh, sháh báshe, áfrin. }	

	Conjunctions.
Blessings=Sad rahmat.	And=Aw.
Amen, so it be=Amin.	If=Kah.
Laughing, cheers=Wáh wáh.	Or, either=Yá.
Oh God=Ai Khudáyah.	Otherwise, if not=Kah nah.
Oh Lord=Ai málikah.	Although=Agar kah, agar chih.
Hurrah=Allah-i allah.	Notwithstanding=Sarah dah de.
Congratulations=Mobárak.	That=Chih.
Safety, peace, good wishes } =Salámat.	But, moreover, even=Lá, balkeh.
	Also=Hum.
Excellent=Akh.	But=Kho, wale, magar, lekin.
Very good=Der khah.	Except, without—Sewá, be lah.
May I sacrifice my life for you = { Qorbán sham, balá de wakhlam }	Then—Báre, nu.
	Because—Wale chih, zakah chih.
Get away, be gone=Lare.	Therefore— { Zakah, pas, de dai párah. }
Be gone, be lost=Wrak shah.	
	Only—Khali, tash, faqat, siraf.
Get away= { Kure, chakhe (applies to dogs). }	Well, then—Jor.

CALENDER.

The months of year in Pashto, Arabic and Hindi, are used by the Pathans :—

Month	1	2	3	4	5	6	7	8	9	10	11	12
Pashto.	Da Hasan Husain miásht.	Safarah.	Wrunbá-i Khor.	Dwayamah Khor.	Dreyamah Khor.	Saloramah Khor.	Da Khudáe miásht.	Shoqadar.	Rozhah.	Warúkai Akhtar,	Da khali miásht or miyánáh	Loe Akhtar.
Arabic.	Moharram.	Safar.	Rabi-ul-Awal.	Rabi-ul-Sáni.	Jamádi-ul-Awal.	Jamádi-ul-Sáni.	Rajab.	Shá Bán.	Ramzán.	Shawál.	Zil Qadah.	Zil Hijjah.
Hindi,	Wisák or Baisák.	Jait.	Hár.	Pashakál.	Bádro	Asú.	Katak.	Magar.	Poh.	Máh.	Pagani.	Chaiter.

NOTE—The Pashto and Arabic months are in common use, but the Hindi months are only use by the farmers as regard the seasons.

The days of week in Pashto and Persian with the English equivalents.

Day.	1	2	3	4	5	6	7
English...	Friday.	Saturday.	Sunday.	Monday.	Tuesday.	Wednesday	Thursday
Pashto ...	Da Júme wraz.	Da Kháli wraz.	Da Itbár wraz.	Da Gul or da Pir wraz.	Da Naheh wraz.	Da Shoru or da Budh wraz.	Ziyárat or da ziyárat wraz.
Persian...	Adinah	Shambah	Yak Shambah.	Dú Shambah.	Seh Shambah.	Chár Shambah.	Panj Shambah.

THE SEASONS.

Season.	1	2	3	4
English ...	Spring.	Summer.	Autumn.	Winter.
Pashto ...	Sparlai, Bohár.	Aorai.	Manai.	Jamai or Zhamai.

THE CHIEF POINTS.

English ...	West.	North.	Soth.	East.
Pashto ...	Qablah, Nwar prewátuh.	Qotab.	Sohel.	Nwar khátuh.

NUMERALS–CARDINALS.

English	1	2	3	4	5	6	7	8	9	10	20
Pashto	Yau.	Dwah	Dre.	Salor.	Pinzuh.	Shpag.	Awuh	Atuh	Nahuh	Las.	Shal.

Prefix the above to the following cardinal for after "10" upto "99".

English.	10	20	30	40	50	60	70	80	90
Pashto.	Las.	Wisht.	Dersh.	Salwikht	Panzos.	Shpetuh	Awiyá.	Atiyá.	Nwi.

NOTE 1—13 should be read "Dyár las", 14=Swárlas", 16="Shpáras", & 19="Núlas".

NOTE 2—All cardinals with exception of "yau" (one) are unchangeable in the oblique cases of singular, but they take the addition of "o" in the oblique cases of plural after dropping their final "ah" and "uh" as :—"dwah" (2) "dwao" (by two etc.)

NOTE 3—Yau (one) declined like an ordinal number.

NOTE 4—Some Pathans instead of "salwikht" (40) say "Dwah shalah" (two scores) and so on.

Above 99.

English ...	100	1,000	100,000	30,000,000
Pashto ...	Sal.	Zar.	Lak.	Kror.
Plural.	Hundreds.	Thousands.	Lacs.	Crors.
	Sawah or Salgúna.	Zarah or Zargúnah.	Lakah or Lakúnah.	Krorah or Krorúnah.

Above a hundred, the numbers proceed regularly as :—Yau sal yau (101) and so on

ORDINALS.

Add "am" or "yam" to the cardinals except "awal" (first) as :—
"dwah" (two) "dwayam" (second).

NOTE 1—Those cardinals ending in "e" or "é" take "yam", all others take "am" to form the ordinal.

NOTE 2—The feminine of the ordinal is formed by adding "ah" to them and then declined like the feminine nouns ending in "ah" as "dreyam" (third masculine singular), "dreyamah" (third feminine singular), "dreyame" (by third feminine singular) and so on.

NOTE 3—Those cardinal and ordinal numbers having "ah" or "uh" in the final, drop "ah" or "uh" when joined together or forming the feminine or oblique cases.

DIFFERENT NUMBERS.

Collective.	A pair, couple.	A bullock team.	A score.	Four cowries.	Per cent.	A century.
	Jorah.	Qolbah.	Korá-i.	Gandah.	Sekrah.	Sadá-i.
Distributive.	Repeat the cardinal numbers as :—"yau yau"=one at a time, or one by one.					
Multiplicative.	Use the particle "pah" with the oblique plural of the cardinal numbers as :—"pah salo or salgúno"=in hundreds, when "pah" is placed between the coupled cardinal, it forms the precision :—"dwah pah dwah" (exactly two).					
Duplicative.	Add the words "Braghah" (fold) and "chand" (double) to the cardinals. Sometimes "teh" (fold) is added for clothes etc. as :—"dwah braghah" (two fold) "dú chandah"=as much as twice.					
Universality.	Add the word "wárah" (whole) with the cardinals as :—"dre wárah" (all three).					
Numeral Adverbs.	Add "zal" or "wár" to the cardinals as :—"yau zal, or yau wár" (once).					
Franctional.	$\frac{1}{4}$	$\frac{1}{2}$	$\frac{3}{4}$	$1\frac{1}{4}$	$1\frac{1}{2}$	$1\frac{3}{4}$
	Páo.	Nim.	Dre páwah or páo kam yau.	Páo bánde yau, or pinzah páwah.	Yau nim.	Páo kam dwah.

VERBS.

Verbs are of two kinds and of two classes viz :—

1. Primitive.	These are the simple or original ones and may be either transitive or intransitive as :—*"Kawul" (to do) transitive and "Kedal" (to become) intransitive.
2. Derivative.	These are formed by adding "Kawul" or "Kedal" to nouns and adjectives and these may also be transitive or intransitive. When "Kawul" is added to a noun or an adjective it converts it to a transitive verb and when "Kedal" is added to a noun or adjective it changes it to an intransitive verb.
1. Transitive.	All verbs whether casual, derivative or compound end in "wul" and some end in "al" are also transitive. Primitive transitive in their present tenses take the accusative case, verbs commencing with "Rá", "Dar and war and "wayal" (to tell), "Katai" (to look), "Legal" (to send), and Khatal (to climb) etc. require their objects to be put in the dative case. Verbs "pukhtal" or "pukhtanah kawul" (to ask), "Ghokhtal" (to want) and "Porewatal" (to cross) take the ablative case.
2. Intransitive.†	All verbs end in "edal" and some end in "al" are also intransitive, these generally take the dative or ablative case.

* In forming verbs the "K" of "Kawul" or "Kedal" is often rejected when the combining noun or adjective ends in a consonant.

† The exceptions are "awredal" (to hear), "Blosedal" (to amuse or to cheat) and "Pukhtedal" (to ask). The latter two verbs are of the old Pashto and are now rarely used.

Casual verbs.	These are formed by adding "awul" to the "Root" of all kinds of verbs such as :—"Kenastal" (to sit) "Kenawul" (to make sit). These are generally put in the daitve case.
Compound verbs.	These are formed by conjugating nouns or adjectives with the auxiliary verbs "Kawul" or "Kedal" as :—"Bandúbast" (arrangement) "Bandúbast kawul" (to make arrangement).
Active voice.	It is formed by the agent of a verb in the active voice.
Passive voice.	It is formed by using the past participle of an active or transitive verb with the different tenses of the auxiliary verb "Kedal" (to become).
Verbal nouns.	(A) The verb itself is used as a noun as :—"Tlal" (to go or going). (B) Change the final "al" or "ul" of the verb, whether transitive or intransitive into "ún" for masculine and into "anah" for feminine, sometimes into "uh" as :—"Katal" (to look) "Katún" or Katanahr or "Kátuh"* (looking).

* Verbs having short "a" in their syllables this "a" must be changed into long "áe before adding the termination "uh" to form the verbal noun.

Noun of fitness	It is formed by putting a verb of the oblique plural into the Genitive case as .—"Da khwaralo" (of eating).
Adverbial phrase.	It is formed by putting the preposition "Sarah" (with) before, sometimes after, a verb in the oblique plural of the Genitive case as :—"Sarah da khlásawulo" (just, on finishing or firing).
Infinitives.	All infinitives in Pashto end in "al", "ul" and "edal".

ROOTS.

The Root of a verb is formed by one of the following ways viz:—

EXAMPLES.

Rule.	How formed.	Infinitive.	Root.
A	*Primitive transitive and intransitive verbs whose infinitives end in "al" & "ul" form their Roots by merely dropping "ul" or "al" :	Legdawul = to load. Sátal = to keep.	(i) Legdaw. (ii) Sát
B	Derivative transitive verbs, the infinitives of which end in "ul", have two forms of their roots. Their first root is formed by merely dropping "ul" of the infinitive and the second root is formed by changing their final "awal" into "kar" as :—	Jorawul = to make	(i) Joraw. (ii) Jor kar.
C	Derivative intransitive verbs whose infinitives end in "dal" have also two forms of their roots. The first root is formed by changing their final "dal" into "g" and the second root is formed by changing their final "edal" into "sh" as :—	Joredal = to be made or become well.	(i) Joreg. (ii) Jorsh.

* Some primitive verbs having "atal" for the last part, change "atal" into "úz" for root as :—"watal" (to go out) Root "wúz". Primitive verbs having "khtal" in the last part change "khtal" into "r" as :—Nghakhtal (to roll up) Root "nghár" and those *Primitive verbs ending in "stal" or "shtal" change these endings for "l" for roots as :—"Ráwastal" (to bring animate) root "Ráwal".

*If the above endings be preceded by a long vowel this long vowel should be dropped.

The exceptions to the preceding foot note are :—

Verb.	Root.	Verb.	Root.
Tlal = to go.	Z, or lársh	Khatal = to climb.	Khej.
Rátlal = to come.	Ráz or rásh.	Kenástal = to sit.	Ken.
Botlal = to take away or lead (animate).	Boz.	Skakhtál = to cut out a cloth for making dress	Skanr.
Pránastal = to open.	Pránaz.	Wishtal = to shoot.	Wol.
Katal = to look.	Gor.	Ghokhtal = to want.	Ghwár.
Waistal = to expel.	Aobás.	Aghústal = to wear.	Aghúnd.
Aistal = to extract.	Aobás.	Nkhatal = to be stuck.	Nkhal.
Samlástal = to lie down	Samal.	Kanastal = to dig.	Kan.

NOTE 1—The Root of the auxiliary verb "kawul" (to do) is "kaw" or "kar" and "kedal" (to become) is "keg" or "sh".

NOTE 2—The Roots of the compound verbs must be obtained from their last verb; and the last or principal verb is only subject to conjugation in such cases.

The Root of the following verbs are formed by merely dropping their final "edal" :—

Verb.	Root.	Verb.	Root.
To dwell = Aosedal.	Aos.	To run = Zghaledal.	Zghal.
To exist (animate) = Páedal.	Pá.	To flee = Takhtedal.	Takht.
To hear = Awredal.	Awr.	To move = Khwazedal.	Khwaz.
To rise = Pásedal.	Pás.	To fly = Alúzedal.	Alúz.
To arrive = Rasedal.	Ras.	To wheel = Chúrledal.	Chúrl.
To appear = Khkáredal.	Khkár.	To roll = Ragharedal.	Rghar.
To shine = Brekhedal.	Brekh.	To wander = Garzedal.	Garz.
To bathe = Lambedal.	Lamb.	To swing = Zangedal.	Záng.
To be entangled = Nkhaledal.	Nkhal.	To quiver = Regdedal.	Regd.
To burn = Swazedal.	Swaz.	To graze = Saredal.	Sar.
To leak = Sasedal.	Sás.	To be stuck To effect To commence To be spent } = Lagedal.	Lag.
To be shed (flower) = Rashedal	Razh.	To draw apart = Lwaredal.	Lwar.

The Root of the following verbs are formed by rejecting their last "dal" :—

Verb.	Root.	Verb.	Root.
To recognise=Pejandal.	Pejan.	To find=Mundal.	Múm.
To undo, unfold=Spardal or Sparodal.	Spar.	To weave=Aodal.	Aw.
To suck=Raodal.	Raw.	To split=Cháodal.	Chaw.
To swallow=Nghardal.	Nghar.	To dig=Kanodah.	Kan.

NOTE—In the above verbs the "n" in "Mundal" must be changed into "m"; and change the "o" in "Raodal", "Aodal" and "Cháodal" into "w". The "o" in Sparodal and "Kanodal" should also be dropped when forming the root.

The following verbs form their root irregularly :—

Verb.	Root.	Verb.	Root.
To catch=Niwal.	Nis.	To turn out=Aokhkal.	Aokág.
To put or to place=Ekhodal or Kekhodal.	Ked, or kegd or gd.	To let go, allow=Prekhodal.	Pregd.
To take away (inanimate) } Wral.	Yos or wr.	To pull=Rákhkal.	Bákág.
To knead=Akhal.	Aghag.	To see=Lidal.	Win.
To vomit=Járestal or Járbasal.	Járbás.	To lead=Biwul.	Biyá.
To kill=Wajal.	Wajn.	To rub=Makhal.	Mag.

Past Participle	It is always of the masculine gender and singular number, and declining like a masculine noun ends in "ai". Its feminine singular or plural is formed by changing the final "ai" into "e".

It is formed as follows :—

Rule	How formed.	Infinitive.	Past Participle.
A	Primitive transitive & intransitive verbs the infinitives of which end in "al" or "ul", form their past participle by adding "ai" to the infinitive :—	Niwal, to catch.	Niwalai.
B	Derivative transitive verbs whose infinitives end in "ul", form their past participle by changing their last "awul" into "karai" :—	Jorawul, to make.	Jor karai.
C	Derivative intransitive verbs whose infinitives end in "dal", form their past participle by changing their last "edal" into "shawai" :—	Khabredal, to be informed.	Khabar shawai.

NOTE—The past participle of the auxiliary verbs 'kawul' (to do) is "karai", and "kedal" (to become) is "shawai".

Present Participle.	In Pashto it is used as a noun and formed by changing "al" and "ul" of the infinitive into "uh" for masculine, and into "ah" for feminine as :—"Pohedal" (to understand) " Poheduh " masculine, 'Pohedah" feminine (understanding).

Particles.	Positive particle.	Prohibitive particle.	Aorist particle.	Future particle.	Conditional particle.
	Wu=so be it.	Mah=don't.	Wi=may be, exists.	Bah=will.	Kah=if.

The following adjectives are commonly used with the different tenses of the auxiliary verbs "kawul" and "kedal", instead of their verbs :—

Masculine.	Feminine.	Masculine.	Feminine.
Nást=sitting.	Nástah.	Mlást=lying.	Mlástah.
Walár=standing.	Walarah.	Prot=lying.	Pratah.

PERSONAL AFFIXES.			PRONOMINAL SUFFIXES.		
Person.	Singular.	Plural.	Person.	Singular.	Plural.
1st.	am.	ú.	1st.	am.	ú.
2nd.	ai.	a-i.	2nd.	ai.	á-i.
3rd (M.)	i.	i.	3rd (M.)	uh.	(Infinitive alone).
3rd (F.)	i.	i.	3rd (F.)	ah.	e.

THE PRESENT AUXILIARY TENSE.
SINGULAR.
I am = Zuh yam.

Thou art = Tuh yai.

He, it, or that is = Haghah dai.

She is = Haghah dah.

PLURAL.
We are = Múng yú.

You are = Táso yá-i.

They are = Haghoe di.

There are two other forms of the 3rd Person Present tense which are also used, as :—

He, it, that, or she is. } Haghah shtah* or yee | They are = Haghoe shtah or yee.

*"Shtah" and "yee" (is, or are), are the real present auxiliary tenses of the 3rd person, both singular and plural, masculine and feminine. Their places have been taken by "dai", "dah" (is), and "di" (are) which are in commoner use than "shtah" or "yee". The form "shtah" is more emphatic than the forms "dai", "dah" or "di"; "shtah" is generally used with interrogative sentences, or in asking questions as :—"Haghah daltah shtah" (is he here) "nah nishtah" (no he is not here). "Shtah" often takes "dai", "dah" or "di", when more emphasis is intended as :—"Haghah haltah shatah dai"=(certainly), he is there). "Yee" is generally used with the 3rd persons of the auxiliary future and aorist tenses, where it becomes "wi".

"Wi" or "yee" mean exists and they also denote duration and probability.

"Shtah", "dai", "dah", or "di", are used for certainty while "wi" or "yee" are used to express doubt.

THE FUTURE AUXILIARY TENSE.

SINGULAR.	PLURAL.
I will·be = Zuh bah yam.	We will be = Múng bah yú.
Thou wilt be = Tuh bah yai.	You will be = Táso bah yá-i.
He, she, it, or that will-be } = Haghah bah yee or wi	They will be = { Haghoe bah yee or wi.

THE AORIST AUXILIARY TENSE.

SINGULAR.	PLURAL.
He, she, it, or that may be } = Haghah yee or wi.	They may be = Haghoe yee or wi.

NOTE—The aorist auxiliary tense has the third person singular and plural tense only.

THE PAST AUXILIARY TENSE.

SINGULAR.	PLURAL.
I was = Zuh wam.	We were = Múng wú.
Thou wast = Tuh wai.	You were = Táso wá-i.
He was = Haghah wuh.	They were = Haghoe wú.
She was = Haghah wah.	They (f.) were = Haghoe we.

THE PAST HABITUAL AUXILIARY TENSE.

SINGULAR.	PLURAL.
I used to be = Zuh bah wam.	We used to be = Múng bah wú.
Thou used to be = Tuh bah wai.	You used to be = Táso bah wá-i.
He used to be = Haghah bah wuh.	They used to be = Haghoe bah wú.
She used to be = Haghah bah wah.	They (f.) used to be } = Haghoe bah we

38

THE PAST CONDITIONAL AUXILIARY TENSE.

SINGULAR.	PLURAL.
If, I had been = Kah zuh wai.	If, we had been = Kah múng wai.
If, thou hadst been = Kah tuh wai.	If, you had been = Kah táso wai.
If, he or she had been } = Kah haghah wai.	If, they had been = { Kah haghoe wai.

The tenses of the verb Shwal (to be or to be able).

Person.	PRESENT TENSE. Singular.	PRESENT TENSE. Plural.	Person.	PAST TENSE. Singular.	PAST TENSE. Plural.
1st.	Sham.	Shú.	1st.	Shwam.	Shwú.
2nd.	Shai.	Shá-i.	2nd.	Shwai.	Shwá-i.
3rd. (M.)	Shi.	Shi.	3rd. (M.)	Shwuh.	Shwal.
3rd. (F.)	Shi.	Shi.	3rd. (F.)	Shwah.	Shwe.

NOTE—The above are never used alone as they must be added to the past participle of another verb to form the potential tenses.

TENSES.

The chief tenses are 9 in number, 3 are used for Present and 6 for Past times, but with the addition of some common ones they are made upto 15, and are formed as follows :—

TENSES FORMED FROM INFINITIVE.

Infinitive Mood "Kawul" or "Kral" (to do), and "Kedal" or "Shwul" (to become).

Mood.	No.	Tense.	How formed.	Examples.
Infinitive.	1	*Noun of Agency.	Change the final "al" or "ul" of the infinitive into "únkaı", sometimes into "únai".	(i) Kawúnkai, or Kawúnai = the doer. (ii) Kedúnkai, or Kedúnai = the becomer.
	2	Past Imperfect.	In transitive verbs, use the infinitive alone, and the verb must agree with the object, and change the nominative into agent. In intransitive verbs, add the Pronominal Suffixes, and the verb must agree with the subject.	(i) Má kawul = I was doing. (ii) Zuh kawulam = Thou etc. wast, or were doing me. (iii) Zuh kedamt = I was becoming.
	3	Past Tense.	Prefix ‡"wu" to the Past Imperfect:	(i) Tá wukral§ = Thou didst (ii) Tuh wukrai = I etc. did thee. (iii) Tuh wushwai = Thou became.
	4	Continuative Past or Past Habitual.	Use "bah" with the Past Imperfect:	(i) Haghuh bah kawul = He used to do (ii) Haghah bah kawuluh = I etc. used to do him. (iii) Haghah bah keduh = He used to become.

*To add "wállah" to the infinitive of the oblique plural, or to a noun for the noun of agency is more like Hindustani, though it is seldom used as :—"Kawulo wállah" (the doer), "Imtehán wállah" (the Examiner).

†The "L" of "Kedal" in all Past tenses is often dropped.

‡Some verbs do not admit the Prefix of "wu", therefore their infinitives alone are used in the Past tenses as :—Kenástal (to sit or they sat down).

§The "R" in "wukral" does not sound in the course of conversation.

1 (*a*). Derivative transitive verbs having "Kawul" or "awul" for the last Part, change "kawul" or "awal" into "kral" in all Past tenses except in Noun of Agency, Past Imperfect and Continuative Past or Past Habitual, where "kawul", "awul" or "kral" may either be used.

(*b*). Derivative intransitive verbs having "kedal" or "edal" in the last part, change "kedal" or "edal" into "shwal" in all Past tenses except in Noun of Agency, Past Imperfect, and Continuative Past or Past Habitual, where "kedal", "edal" or "shwal" may either be used.

2 (*c*). In Transitive verbs, in all Past tenses, the verb agrees in gender, number and case with the object, and the nominative is changed into agent, therefore in the first examples of the above tenses, the verb is put in 3rd Person masculine plural, because no object is mentioned.

(*d*). In the Pashto language, when no object is mentioned, the verb is put in 3rd Person masculine plural.

(*e*). In the 2nd examples of the above tenses, the persons are shown in the objective form.

3 (*f*). In Intransitive verbs, in all Past tenses, the verb agrees in gender, number and case with the object, and the nominative remains unchanged, therefore in the 3rd examples of the above tenses, the persons are shown in the subjective form.

TENSES FORMED FROM ROOT.

Mood.	No.	Tense.	How formed.	Examples.
Imperative.	1	Indefinite Imperative.	Add "ah" for singular person, and á-i for plural person, to the Root :—	(i) *Kawah (do thou), Kawá-i (do you). (ii) Kegah (become thou), Kegá-i (become you).
		Definite Imperative.	Prefix †"wu" to the Indefinite Imperative:	(i) ‡Wukrah (do thou), Wukrá-i (do you). (ii) Wushah (become thou), Wushá-i (become you).
Indicative.	2	Present Tense.	Add Personal Affixes to the Root :—	(i) Zuh kawam=I do, or am doing. (ii) Múng kegú=(we become, or we are becoming).
	3	Indefinite Future.	Use §"bah" with the Present Tense :—	(i) Tuh bah kawaí= (thou shall do). (ii) Táso bah kegá-i= (you shall become).
	4	Aorist Tense.	Prefix 'wu" to the Present Tense, and place ‖"di" before the prefixed "wu" for the 3rd person singular and plural :—	(i) Táso wukrá-i=(you may do). (ii) Haghah di wushi, or wu di shi=(he or she may become).
	5	Definite Future.	Use "bah" before the Aorist Tense. "Di" (3rd person aorist) is never used with this tense :—	(i) Haghah bah wukri, or wu bah kri=(he or she will do). (ii) Haghoe bah wushi, or wu bah shi=(they will become).

* The Root "kaw" of "kawul" and "keg" of "kedal", are used with the Indefinite Imperative, Present, and Indefinite Future tenses.

† Verbs which do not take the Prefix of the Positive Particle "wu", have no definite Imperative in the Positive form; but the Prohibitive Particle "mah" may be prefixed instead of "wu" for the negative sense as :—"jorawul" (to make), "mah jorawah" (don't make).

‡ The Root "kr" of "kral", instead of "kaw" and "sh" of "shwal" instead of "keg" are used in the Definite Imperative, Aorist, and Definite Future of the above tenses.

§ The Future Particle "bah", precedes the prefixed "wu"; but when a personal pronoun is not used with the future, "bah" is placed after "wu'.

‖ "Di" of the third person aorist tense is placed after "wu" when a third person pronoun is not used with the aorist tense.

NOTE—Verbs, especially the intransitive, which do not admit the Prefix of "wu" in Definite Imperative, do not Prefix it in the aorist either.

The following verbs do not take the Prefix of "wu" viz :—

[a] Verbs with the Prefix of the Prohibitive Particle "mah".

[b] Verbs commencing with the dative particles "Rá", "Dar" and "War".

[c] Most of the verbs beginning with two double consonants.

[d] "Botlal" or "Bival" (to lead), "wral" (to carry) and "kekhodal" (to put or to place), and some other transitive and intransitive verbs do not take the Prefix of "wu"

TENSES FORMED FROM PAST PARTICIPLE.

Mood.	No.	Tense.	How formed.	Examples.
Indicative.	1	Past Perfect.	Add the Present auxiliary tense, to the Past Participle :	(i) Má karai dai=(I have done). (ii) Zuh karai yam=[thou etc. have done me]. (iii) Zuh shawai yam=[I have become].
	2	*Future Perfect.	Add the future auxiliary tense, to the Past Participle :	(i) Tá kari bah wi=[thou will, shall, or may have done]. (ii) Tuh karai bah yai=[I etc. will, shall, or may have done thee]. (iii) Tuh shawai bah yai=[thou will, shall, or may have become]
	3	Plu-Perfect.	Add the Past auxiliary tense, to the Past Participle :—	(i) Haghuh kari wú=[he had done]. (ii) Haghah karai wuh=[I etc. had done him]. (iii) Haghah shawai wuh=[he had become].
Subjunctive.	4	Past Conditional.	Use †"kah" with Plu-Perfect :—	(i) Kah Haghe karai wai=[if, she had done] (ii) Kah haghah karai wah=[if, I etc. had done her]. (iii) Kah haghah shawai wah=[if, she had become].
	5	‡Following Conditional.	Change "kah" of the Past conditional into "nu" (then), and use "bah" before its verb :—	(i) Nu múng bah karai wai =[then, we would or should have done]. (ii) Nu múng bah kari wú =[then, thou etc. would or should have done us]. (iii) Nu múng bah shawi wú=then, we would or should have become].

TENSES FORMED FROM PAST PARTICIPLE—*Contd.*

Mood	No.	Tense.	How formed.	Examples.
Potential.	6	§Present Potential.	Add the Present tense of "shwal" to the Past Participle :	(i) Táso ‖kawulai shá-i = (you can do). (ii) Táso kedalai shá-i = (you can become).
	7	Future Potential.	Use "bah" with the Present Potential :	(i) Haghoe bah kawulai shi = (They will be able to do). (ii) Haghoe bah kedalai shi = (they will be able to become).
	8	Past Potential.	Add the Past tense of "shwal" to the Past Participle :—	(i) Haghoe kawulai shwat = they could do). (ii) Haehoe kawulai shwe = (I etc. could do them (f.) (iii) Haghoe kedalai shwe = (they (f.) could become).

* The Future Perfect is also called the Future Past, or the Doubtful Past.

† The Conditional Particle "Kah" (if), may be placed before, sometimes after the Chief Pronoun in all tenses of the Present, or Past times to form the Conditional tenses.

‡The Following Conditional tense, always follows and answers the Conditional tense.

§ The Present, and Future Potential, and all tenses of the Present and Future times have no objective form.

‖ As a rule "Kawulai" and "Kedalai" are the inflected forms of "Kawul" and "Kedal", and are used in the places of their Past Participles "Krai" and "Shawai", throughout the Potential tenses, especially by Yúsufzá-is.

Note—The Tense which indicates regret, desire, etc. is formed by adding the Past Habitual auxiliary tense to a Past Participle, as :—Zuh bah talai wai (had I gone); sometimes "Kashki" or "Dreghah" (would to God), and other interjections are placed instead of the Future Particle "bah" to form the above tenses.

IRREGULAR VERBS.

No	Infinitive,	Root.	Past Participle.
1	To be or to exist = *yal	Y.	None.
2	To be or to be able = Shwal	Sh.	Shawai.
3	To go = †Tlal or Láral.	‡Z. or Lársh.	Talai.
4	To come = Rátlal or Rághlal	Ráz or Rásh.	Rághalai.
5	To come to thee or to you = Dartlal or Dar raghlal.	Darz or Darsh.	Dar rághalai.
6	To go to him, to her, or to them = Wartlal or War raghlal.	Warz or Warsh.	War rághalai.
7	To have = Laral.	Lar.	Laralai.

* "Yal" is an old Pashto verb not now in use, and its verbal noun is shtah or shtanah = (being, existence).

† "Tlal" is the only principle verb, and it forms the other verbs of "coming" and "going" by Prefixing the Dative Particles "Rá", "Dar", and "War"; each of these verbs have two infinitives and two Roots, the first form of their infinitives are used as their real verbs, and the second form of their infinitives are used in all their Past and Perfect tenses except "Tlal" which takes its second infinitive "Láral" in the Past tense, and its regular Past Participle "Talai" is used in its Perfect tenses.

‡ The second root of all the verbs of "coming" and "going" is more emphatic than the first ones, and it is generally used in their aorist tenses.

NOTE—The Prohibitive "mah" is only used with the roots "Z", "Ráz", and "Warz" all the other roots of the verbs of "coming" and "going" take the negative "nah" in the Imperative.

USE OF IRREGULAR VERBS.

Imperative.	Present.	Future.	Aorist.	Past.	Perfect.
Yal., be thou, or exist thou. Yá-i, be you, or exist you.	Yam, (I) am	Bah yai, You (thou) will be.	Di yi or wi di, He, she or they may be, or may exist.	Wú, (We, you or they) were, or been, or existed.	(*)
† Kawulai sham, I can do.	Kawulai shai, You (thou) can do.	Bah kawulai shi, He or she or they will be able to do.	Kawulai di shi, He, she or they may do.	Kawulai shwal, They could do.	(‡)
[Indefinite] Zah, go thou. [Definite] Lárshah, go thou.	Zi, He, or she goes, or they go.	Bah zi, He, she or they will go.	Zi di or lár di shi, He, she or they may go.	Láralú or Lárú, We went.	Tali yá-i, You have gone.
[Indefinite] Rázah, come thou. [Definite] Ráshah, come you.	Rázam, I come.	Bah rázai, Thou will come.	Rázi di, or Rá di shi, He, she or they may come.	Rághlú, We came.	Rághali yá-i, You have come.
§ [Indefinite] Dar zi di, He, she or they should come to thee or to you. [Definite] Dar di shi, He, she or they must come to thee or to you.	Darzam, I am coming or come to thee or to you.	Bah dar zi, He, she or they will come to thee or to you.	Dar zi di or Dar di shi, He, she or they may come to thee or to you.	Dar rághalam or Dar rágham, I came to thee or to you.	Dar rághalai dai, He has come to thee or to you.
[Indefinite] War zah, go to him or to her or to them. [Definite] War shah, go to him or to her or to them.	War zi, He goes to him or to her or to them.	Bah warzú, We will go to him or to her or to them.	War zi di or War di shi, He, she or they may go to him or to her or to them.	War rághlam or War rágham, I went to him or to her or to them.	War rághali yú, We have gone to him or to her or to them.

Verb "yal" has no Perfect tenses, because it has no Past Participle.

† The verb "to be able" has no Imperative mood. It is supplied by its Present or Aorist tenses.

‡ The verb "to be able" cannot be used in the Perfect tenses.

§ Verb "Dartlal" has also no regular Imperative, its place is taken by the Present or Aorist tenses of the verb.

NOTE—Like other Particles the 3rd Person Aorist Particle "di" is also placed after the Prefixed "Lár", "Rá", "Dar" and "War" of the second roots of the Aorist tense of all the above verbs of "coming" and "going."

USE OF THE VERB "TO HAVE".

The verb "to have" means "Laral", it is generally translated by "shtah" (is or are), dai, or dah (is), and "di", (are) the third Persons of the Present auxiliary tense.

(*a*) "Laral" (to have), is conjugated like other transitive verbs as :—"Zuh nokar laram" (I have a servant).

(*b*) When the verb "to have" is expressed by *"shtah", or "dai", or "dah", or "di", the subject must be put in the genitive case, as :— "Zmakah di shtah"? or "stá zmakah shtah"? ("Have you land"?).

(*c*) If †"sakhah" (with, or in possession of) is preceded by a pronoun or a noun, "shtah", "dai", "dah", or "di", do not require their subject to be put in the genitive case, as :—"múng sakhah topakúnah nishta" (We have no rifles).

* "Shtah" is often combined with "dai", or "dah" or "di", for certainty, as :—"as mi shtah dai" (Certainly, I have a horse).

† "Sakhah" is the corruption of "sarah" (with), with the verb "to have" it is used for irrational beings and movable objects; in ordinary sense it is used for both rational beings, as well as for irrational beings, movable as well as immovable objects, and it is never used with the verb "to have" when speaking of sicknesses.

MISCELLANEOUS RULES.

CASES,

I. These are eight viz :—

No.	Case.	How formed	No.	Case.	How formed
1	Nominative	It is a simple form of a noun.	5	Accusative.	Same as the nominative, it remains uninflected.
2	Agent.	Simple *inflection of noun.	6	Ablative.	Put the inflected noun between the preposition "lah-nah" (from).
3	Genitive.	Place the preposition "da" (of), before the inflected noun.	7	Locative.	Place the inflected noun between the prepositions "pah-ke" (in), or "pah-bánde" (on), or tre-pore (upto).
4	Dative.	Put the preposition "tah" (to), after the inflected noun.	8	Vocative.	Place the interjection "ai", or "ao" (oh), before the inflected noun and add "ah" after it.

* Inflected nouns mean only those masculine and feminine nouns which are subject to inflection in the oblique cases of the singular, all others remain unchanged, except in the oblique cases of plural nouns, where they take the addition of ' u '. Vide page 9.

FORMATION OF SENTENCES.

II. To form a sentence, as a general rule the pronoun must be put in first, then the noun* and lastly the verb i. e. the subject first, the object second, and the verb last.

III. In Pushto there is no sign of the object of a sentence, it may be known by its place after the agent before the verb as :— "má spaï wuwajaluh" (I killed the dog).

IV. In interrogative sentences when an interrogative pronoun is not used, the words "Kah nah." (if, not, or not), sometimes "sah" (what? is it?) are added to the last verb as :—"war yi kral kah nah" (Did he give it him or not?;). "Lah pekhawar nah rághlal sah" (Did they come from Peshawar?). The above words however, are not necessary, as the tone of voice is enough to indicate interrogation.

V. In addressing the second person plural, the Pathans use the second person singular, except when addressing more than one man, or a respectable person as :—"Chartah wai"=*Where were you? (lit. Where wast thou?)

VI. When a Possessive Pronoun in a sentence, refers to its subject, it must be translated by the reflexive pronoun "Khpal" (own) as :—"Alam Khan khpal kár wukaruh" (Alam Khan did his own work).

NARRATION.

VII. The narration is expressed in Pushto by using the same words as were used by the speaker or were supposed to have been used, i. e. by using the first person singular or plural instead of the third person which made use of the words or action as :—"Haghah wuwaï chih bah rásham (He said that he would come). The indirect narration is not allowed, but however it is expressed by placing the Conjunctive "chih" between two sentences as :—"Haghah wuwaï chih tuh daroghjan yai" (He said, "I was a liar").

VIII. The Present or Past tense is often used for future as :— "Pah balah miásht ke rawánegú" (We will start (starting) next month), "Kah di rawaruh no inám wákhlah" (If you will bring (brought) it, you will get the reward).

XI. The Past Participle is also used as a Conjunctive Particle as :—' Mlá taralai rawán shuh" (Having fastened his waist he started off).

XI. A meaningless apposite word is often added to a noun for euphony or better sound. It is obtained by repeating a noun and changing the first letter of the second noun into "m"; sometimes into "w" or "p" as :—"Obuh mbuh" (water and other liquid).

---

* When a noun requires an adjective, or a verb or an adverb, the former must precede while the latter must follow the noun.

EXERCISES.

— o —

EXERCISE I.

ORAL.

The khán's followers = Da khán mlátarán.
In the army = Pah fauz ke.
On the hill = Pah ghar bánde.
By the soldiers = Spáhiáno.
To the war = Jang tah.
From the country = Lah mulk nah.
Up to the fort = Tre qlá pore.
Oh! Pathan! = Ai pukhtúnah.

My father = Zamá plár, or plár mi.
Your (thy) mother = Stá mor, or mor di.
His brother = Da haghuh wror, or wror yi.
Her sister = De haghe khor, or khor yi.

Our parents = Zamúng mor plár, or mor plár mu.
Your uncle = Staso truh, or truh mu.
Their cousins = Da haghoe tarbúrán, or tarburán yi.

Their forefathers = Da haghoe plár nikúnah, or plár nikúnah yi.

I am a Pathan = Zah pukhtún yam.
You (thou) are an Indian = Tuh hinkai yai.
He is a European = Haghah ferangai dai.
She is a Punjabi = Haghah Punjábá-i dah.
We are Yusafzá-is = Múng Yusafzi yú.
You are Afridis = Táso Afridi yá-i.
They (m.) are Khataks = Haghoe Khatak di.
They (f.) are Mahmunds = Haghoe Mahmundáni di.

I was ill = Zah nájrah wam.
You (thou) were well = Tah jor wai.
Where was he? = Haghah chartah wuh.
She was at home = Haghah kor wah.
We were there = Múng haltah wú.
You were here = Táso daltah wá-i.
They (m.) were absent = Haghoe ghair házir wú, or maujúd nah 'wú.
They (f.) were busy = Haghoe wúzgáre nah we, or haghoe lagyá we.

This is a good and great man = Dá khuh aw loe sarai dai.

That is a very bad place = Haghah der kharáp záe dai.

These men are old, short, lazy, ignorant and ugly = Dá sari záruh or spingiri, jak or madri, nárástah, kamakal or jáhilán, aw badrangah di.

Those women are young, tall, smart, intelligent and handsome = Haghah khaze zwánáne, dange, chábake, hokhiáre aw kháyistah or khkole di.

EXERCISE 1.

WRITTEN.

I am a Pathan. My father was a Pathan. You are a bad man. He was a great man. She was a good woman. This boy is the Khan's son. That girl is the headman's daughter. This old man is our grand father. That old woman is your grand mother. This short man is that young man's uncle. That tall woman is this young boy's mother. These men are their cousins. Those men were their forefathers. This boy is the girl's brother. That girl is the boy's sister. He is handsome but she is ugly. The man is the woman's husband. The woman is the man's wife. He is ignorant but she is intelligent. This man and that woman are good. My brother's sons are good boys. Your sister's daughters are bad girls. The boy is lazy but the girl is smart. His grand-children are very handsome but their parents are very ugly. Their husbands are lazy, ignorant and ugly, but their wives are smart, intelligent and handsome.

---o---

EXERCISE 2.

ORAL.

This (m) is good = Dá khuh dai.

That (m) is bad = Haghah nákárah or kharáp dai.

This (f) is better = Dá khah dah or derah khah dah.

It (f) is worse = Haghah nákárah, or kharápah dah.

These (m) are the best = Dá lah tolo nah khuh or ghwarah di.

Those (m) are the worst = Haghah lah tolo nan nákárah or kharáp or badtar di.

This man is better than that man = Dá sarai lah haghe sari nah khuh dai.

These men are worse than animals = Dá sari lah zanáwaro nah badtar di.

Those women are worse than dogs = Haghah khaze lah spo nah badtare di.

He is the strongest, bravest, handsomest and wisest of all= Haghah lah tolo nah tandrast or mazbút or takrah, zruhwar or túrzan, kháyistah or per makhe, pobah or hokhiár dai.

She is the weakest, ugliest, most ignorant, and most cowardly of all=Haghah lah tolo nah kamzore, badrangah or nákárah, kamakhlah aw be zruh dah.

───────

The horse is bigger, younger and swifter than the mare=As lah aspe nah loe, zwán aw garandai dai.

The mare is smaller, weaker and slower than the horse=Aspah lah as nah warah or waroke, kamzore aw wro dah.

───────

The King's palace is the largest and strongest of all the houses in the city=Da bádsháh mánrá-i da khár lah korúno nah loeah, aw pakhah or chúnah gat dah.

The khan's bungalow is higher and stronger than the village houses =Da khan hawellá-i da kali lah korúno nah úchatah or haskah aw pakhah dah.

The village houses are lower and are built of mud=Da kali korúnah wárah or khkatah or kúz aw kachah di.

───────

EXERCISE 2.
WRITTEN.

The Rifle is a better weapon than the Sword. The Revolver is the best of all weapons and the knife is the worst of all. My father was stronger and braver than your father. His mother is smarter and wiser than their mother. This man's horse is stronger and swifter than that soldier's mare. That woman's mare is weaker and slower than this man's horse. The soldier is the strongest and bravest but most ignorant of all and the servant is the weakest and most cowardly but wisest of all. This boy is older and lazier than those boys. That girl is younger and handsomer than these girls. These (m) are the newest and most beautiful of all. Those (f) are the oldest and worst of all. The farmers houses are bigger than the village houses. This is the largest and best of all.

─────o─────

EXERCISE 3.
ORAL.

Who are you ?=Tuh sok yai.

Whose son are you ?=Da chá zoe yai.

Which woman was she ?=Haghah kumah khazah wah.

How is that man ?=Haghah sarai sah rangah dai.

Who are these men ?=Da sari sok di.

Is he a chief or a headman ?=Haghah khán kah malak dai.

What thing is this ?=Da sah siz or shai dai.

What country does he belong to? (of which country is he?) =
Haghah da kum mulk dai.

He belongs to Tangi = Haghah da Tangi dai.

What kind of place is Tangi? Tangai sah rangah zai dai.

How many houses are there? Hultah somrah korúnah di.

Whose house is this? Dá da chá kor dai.

It is the Arbab Sahib's = Dá da Arbab Sáhib dai.

Which is the Khan's guest house? Da khan hujrah kumah dah.

Will (may) the headman be in the village? Malak pah kali ke
bah wi

He is always (exists) in the city = Haghah múdám pah khár ke wi.

Where were you all yesterday? Táso tol parún chartah wá-i.

Is he employed? (a servant)? Haghah nokar dai.

Is he an infantry or a cavalry soldier? Haghah da paltane spáhi
dai kah da resále sor dai.

He is an artillery man = Haghah da topkháne spáhi dai or
topchi dai

Where is his Regt.? Pathan yi chartah dah.

It is in the Khyber Pass = Pah Khyber darah ke dah.

I have a gun = Rá sakhah topak shtah.

How much money have you? Dar sakhah somrah rupá-i shtah
or di.

Has he a sword = War sakhah túrah shtah.

We have good weapons = Rá sakhah khe wasle di.

How large is your estate? Dar sakhah somrah jáedád dai.

They have much wealth = War sakhah der daulat dai.

EXERCISE 3.
WRITTEN.

Who is this man? Whose son is that boy? Which man was
that one? What is this? How is he? Is he well or ill? Is it good
or bad? Who are those men? They are country chiefs and village
headmen. What place do they belong to (of which place are they?).
They belong to Chamkani. Where is their village? It is near
Peshawar. What sort of place is that? How many houses are
there? Whose guest house is this? Is it the Khan's or the
headman's? It is the Arbab Sahib's. Is he at home (in the house)?
He is not at home. Where may he be now? He is always (exists)
in the city. Will he be in the village tomorrow? Where were all
the servants yesterday? Are you busy or at leisure? Why were
you absent? Are all the soldiers present today? Most are present
but a few are absent. Are you employed (a servant)? What are you
employed in? Are you an Infantry or Cavalry soldier? I am an
Artillery man. Where is your Battery? It is in Risalpur. How
much service have you? Have you a son? Has he any land? He

He has four Persian wells, 160 jeribs of land and 7 Bullock teams.
How much estate had the Khan? He had three villages and much
wealth but no heir. She has no sons but two daughters.

———o———

EXERCISE 4.
ORAL.

The camping ground is very small = Da Paráo medán or dág
der warúkai dai.

The forest near the hill is dense = Ghar sakhah, or ghartah nizde
zangal ganr dai.

The road towards the thick forest is not good = Banr tah or da
banr lár khah nah dah.

The road from Peshawar up to the Khyber pass is good = Lah
Pekhawar nah tre Khyber ghákhi pore lár khah dah.

The road through the valley is bad = Da dare pah meanz ke lár
kharápah or nakárah dah.

The open plain road is unmetalled and dangerous, but the high
road is metalled and safe = Da mere lár kachah aw khatar nákah dah
kho loeah or bádsháhi lár pakhah aw be khofah or be khatarah or
beyare dah.

The Rustam bazar is very populous = Da Rustam bázár der
garam, or abád dai.

Which way is the village? = Kalai pah kum lori or kum khwá dai.

There are numerous people in the King's garden = Bádsháhi
bágh ke der álam or beshánah aúlas dai.

The hilly people are simple but the plain people are cunning =
Da gharúno khalk or gharsani khalk sádah di kho da same khalk
chálákah di.

In Cabul the Bádámi bágh is a marvellous place = Pah Kabal ke
bádámi bágh ajeebah záe dai.

A big fair takes place (exists) at (on) the shrine of Kaka Sahib
every year = Da Káká Sahib pah ziyárat kál pah kál melah wi or lagi.

How far is Chitral from Malakand? = Lah Malakand nah Chitral
somrah láre dai.

———— ————

EXERCISE 4.
WRITTEN.

The plain near the city is very large. The forest near the river
is dense. The road towards the desert is not good. In that thick
forest there are many large trees there. There is a big fort on the
top of the hill. How many men are there under the tree? The
road from here up to the mountain pass is good, but the valley road is
bad. The road through the forest is unmetalled and dangerous, but
the main road is metalled and safe. What is the name of that village?
Which way is the city? The houses of the city are high and beautiful, the markets are large and populous, but the lanes are very

narrow. There are numerous people in the city. The citizens are clever and cunning, but the villagers are ignorant and simple. There are many gardens around the city. The King's garden is a marvellous place; as there are different kinds of animals and birds there. In the minister's garden there are all sorts of fruit trees and flowers there and a fair takes place (exists) there in the spring every Friday. How many horses, ponies, and asses are there on the open plain today? There were many camels, bullocks and mules on the plain near the city yesterday and a. big cattle fair was held at Makri bazar on Friday. There will be a big meeting at (in) the King's garden tomorrow. How far is Cabul from Peshawar?

―――o―――

EXERCISE 5.
ORAL.

1. That man is the doer of this work = Haghah sarai da de kár kawúnkai dai,

This work is to be done (to become) = Dá kár kedúnkai or shwúnkai dai.

Who is the inventor of this thing? = Da de siz or shi rawánawúnkai (the one who make starte) or jorawúnkai (the maker) sok dai.

Who was the founder (the builder) of that village? Da haghe kali abádawúnkai sok wuh.

The king is to arrive (is to reach) = Bádsháh rárasedúnkai dai or ratlúnkai dai (is to come).

The minister is to leave (is to start) = Wazir rawánedúnkai dai or tlunkai dai (is to go).

2. What were you doing? Tá sah kawul.

The Sahib was employing me = Sahib zuh nokar kawulam.

What was happening (becoming) there? = Haltah sah kedal.

The Nawab of Chitral was arriving at Peshawar = Da Chitral Nawab Sahib pekhawar tah rárasedaluh, or ratluh (was coming).

The Khan of Darband was leaving for (to) the Delhi Darbar = Da Darband Khan da Deli Darbar tah rawánedaluh or tlaluh (was going).

3. I did the work = Má kár wukraluh.

The Government employed me = Sarkár zuh nokar kralam.

The work is done (became) = Kár wushwaluh.

I became a corporal = Zuh náik shwalam.

The peon came and went back = Chaprási rághluh aw bertah láraluh.

4. The servant used to do the work = Nokar bah kár kawuluh.

The master used to beat him = Náik bah haghah wahaluh.

It used to happen (to become) often = Dá bah aksar kedal or shwal.

The messenger used to come and go = Astazai or kásid bah tlaluh aw rátlaluh.

54

EXERCISE 5.
WRITTEN.

1. Who is the doer of this work? This work is not to be done (not to become). The inventor of this thing was a clever man. The founder (the builder) of the city was Abad Khan. Akbar the King was the builder (or the maker) of the Attock Fort. His Majesty the Amir of Cabul is to arrive to Ghazni. The Nawab of Dir was to leave for (to) the Delhi Darbar.

2. What was the sahib doing? He was employing me. What was going on (was becoming) there? I was becoming a corporal. The General was arriving and the regiment was leaving.

3. I did the work. The Adjutant enlisted me in the regiment. That work is done (became). I became a Sergeant. The Commanding Officer came to the office. The Adjutant went to the regiment.

4. The servant used to do the work. The master used to beat him. It used to happen (used to become) often. I used to be (used to become) an officer. The orderly used to come and go every day.

———o———

EXERCISE 6.
ORAL.

1. Do work (Indef. Impert. sing.)=Kár kawah.
Do this work (Def. Impert. plu.)=Dá kár wukrá-i.
Don't do so again=Biyá dáse mah kawah.
Be (become) (Def. Impert. sing.)=Kegah, or shah.
Don't be (become) (Def Impert. plu.)=Mah kegà-i or mah sh-á-i.
Go home (to the house) (Indef. Impert. sing.)=Kor tah zah.
Come to the court (Def. Impert. plu)=Kachará-i tah ráshá-i.
Go to the hospital (Def. Impert. sing)=Shafá kháne tah lárshah.
Don't come here=Daltah mah rázah.
Don't go there=Haltah mah zah.

2. What are you doing?=Tah sah kawai.
Doesn't he do the work?=Haghah kár nah kawi.
The case is on (becoming)=Mokademah kegi.
The sahib comes=Sahib rázi.

3. Will you do work?=Tuh kár bah kawai.
What shall become of this?=Da de bah sah kegi, or wushi.
We shall go to the country=Múng mulk or watan tah bah zú.

4. He may do it=Haghah di wukri.
It may be done (may become)=Dá di wushi.
You may go=Tah lárshah.
The Khan may come=Khán di ráshi.

5. The servant will do this=Nokar dá bah wukri.
This work will be done in this way=Da kar dá rang or pah dá shán bah wushi.
He will come=Haghah bah ráshi.
I will go=Zah bah lárshan.

EXERCISE 6.
WRITTEN.

1. Do the work (Indef. Impert. Sing.). First do this (Def. Impert. plu.). Don't do that. Be (become) a man (Def. Impert.). Don't be (become) a fool (Indef. Impert.). Come to my Bungalow. Go to the office. Don't go anywhere else.

2. ! work. Don't you work? What is going on (becoming) there? I go home (to the house). The headman is going to the village. The Khan goes to and comes (goes and comes) from the city every day.

3. We shall do that work. What shall happen (shall become) then? They shall go to the country. When shall you go to the village? I shall go in a day or two.

4. The servant may do this. That work may be done in this way. May I come or may I go? He may come but they may go.

5. The Headman will make (will do) the arrangement. The arrangement will be made (will be done) in that way. The Khan will go to the city tomorrow. The Sahib will come to the village the day after tomorrow.

———o———

EXERCISE 7.
ORAL.

1. He has done the work = Haghah kár karai dai.
    It has been done = Dá shawai dai.
    What has occurred? = Sah shawi di, or pekh shawi di.

2. The servant may have done = Nokar bah kari wi.
    A row may have occurred = Sah jagarah or pasát bah pekh shawai wi.
    The Khan may have started = Khan bah rawán shawai wi.
    The watchman may have arrived = Saukidár bah rasedalai wi.

3. I had done that work = Má haghah kár karai wuh.
    Something had occurred afterwards = Wrasto sah pekh shawi wú.

4. If they had done this = Kah haghoe dá karai wai.
    If that matter had occurred = Kah haghah maámelah pekhah shawai we.

5. If they had done it in this way, it would have been much better = Kah haghoe dáse or pah de shan karai wai nu derah khah bah wai.

6. No one can do this = Dá hesok kawalai nah shi.
    Why can't it be done? Dá wale kedalai nah shi.

7. That man will be able to do that work = Haghah sarai bah haghah kár wukrai shi.
    I will be unable to do it = Zah bah yi wu nah krai sham.

8. Who could do such a hard job? = Dáse grán kár chá kawulai shuh.
    It could not be done = Dá kedalai nah shuh.

EXERCISE 7
WRITTEN.

1. **Have you done that work?** Has the Sahib engaged you? That work has been done. What has happened (has become) in that case? Have you been (have gone) to the Khyber Pass? This man has come from Cabul.

2. That man may have done this work. He may have beaten you. That work may have been done. Something may have happened (have become). He may have left (have started off). They may have arrived (have reached).

3. They had done the work. The Government had employed them. It had been done. What had happened? (had become). He had come but she had gone.

4. If you had done that work. If this work had been done. If this had happened (had become) thus. If I had been (had gone) on active service. If you had come with me.

5. If the recruits had done good work they would have become good soldiers. If the arrangement had been made (had been done) well, The Khan would have been made (had become) the "Khan Bahadur" If the matter had happened in this way, it would have been much better. If you had come, I would have accompanied you.

6. Can you do this work? It cannot be done. Can you go there? Can't he come here?

7. Will you be able to do this? He will be able to make it. The Sahib will not be able to go to the spot. The Khan will be able to come.

8. I could do the work. He could not beat me. That work could not be done. The Khan could come but the Sahib could not go.

---o---

EXERCISE 8.
ORAL.

May you not be tired, Khan = Khan stare mah shai.

What is the news? = Sah hál dai, or sah hál ahwál dai.

Bring a bed and take away the chair = Kat rawrah aw kursá-i yosah.

Place a carpet on the floor = Pah farsh or pah zmakah (on the earth) lamsai or dará-i wáchawah.

Put (place) these things inside = Dá sizúnah dananah kedah.

Let us sit on the bed and eat (some) food = Razah (come) or pregdah chih pah kat kenú aw dodá-i wukhrú.

Who is sitting (seated) on the chair? = Pah kursái sok nást dai.

Do not lie on the carpet = Pah lamsi or dari mah samlah.

Who is lying there under the verandah dará-i? = Da mandáu láude sok prot or mlást dai.

Make the food ready = Dodá-i tayárah kah.

Is the tea ready? = Chá-e tayárah dah kah nah.

It will be ready soon = Zir bah tayárah shi.

Will you drink some (little) milk ? = Pá-i bah skai.

Smoke the pipe = Chilam wuskah.

Have you tobacco ? = Dar sakhah tamákú shtah,

I have, but there is no fire = Ra sakhah shtah kho aor nishtah.

Tell him to freshen the pipe = Wartah wunayah chih chilam tázah kah.

I will give you (some) sweet meat = Zah suh metyá-i bah dar kam.

Give me, don't give him = Má lah rakrah, haghah lah mah warkawah.

Bring the horse and saddle it = As ráwalah aw zin kah, or zin pre wáchawah.

Take away the mare and unsaddle it = Aspah bozah aw zin tre kúz kah (or lare kah).

Water and feed the bullocks = Ghwayáno tah gayáh aw obuh warkah (or obuh kah).

I commend you to God = Pah Khodáe spáralai or da Khodáe pah amán (protection).

EXERCISE 8.
WRITTEN.

Welcome, Khan. Are you well, fresh and happy ? What is all the news ? Call the servant and tell him to bring a chair for the Khan. Put the chair near the bed. Come Khan sit down on the chair. You may lie on the bed. Who is sitting (seated) there on the bed ? Take away the gun and place it under the bed. Make the food ready. When will it be ready ? The food will be ready in a little while. The servant is bringing the food. Eat (some) food, Khan. Do you drink tea ? The tea is ready. Give me some (a little) cold water, that I may drink. May I give you a sweet drink ? (the sweet water i. e. syrup). Give the Khan some sweet meat and fruits. Do you smoke ? Tell the watchman to fill the pipe. Saddle the horse and take the saddle off the mare and take it away to the stable. Water and feed (give fodder to) the horses. Is this grass good ? I will go to the Court as I have an urgent affair (or business). I shall see you again when I come back (or return). Tell the groom to bring my horse. Good bye. So may it be with you.

———o———

EXERCISE 9.
ORAL.

Have you learned Hindustani ? = Hinko di zdah karai dah.

Have you read your friend's letter ? Da ashná chitá-i di lwastalai dah.

Have you seen the city of Peshawar ? De Pekhawar khár di lidalai dai kah nah.

I have been (have gone) as far as (up to) Nowshera = Da Nokhár pore talai yam.

Have you heard any fresh news ?=Sah tázah khabar di awredalai dai.

The messenger has come from the village=Astázai lah kali nah rághalai dai.

He has brought news of the Khan=Haghuh da Khán khabar ráwarai dai.

He says that the Khan has become ill=Haghah wayi chih Khán najorah shawai dai.

What village is that ?=Haghah kum kalai dai.

It is Torú ?=Torú dai.

Who is the khan of it ?=Khán yi sok dai.

Is he a rich man ?=Haghah mor or daulatmand sarai dai.

He has lots of land and has built many guest houses and Mosques=Haghah derah zmakah or mulk lari aw dere hujre aw júmátúnah yi abád kari di.

The old Khan was a very respectable and influential man = Mashar Khan der izat dárah aw makháwriz or barakati sarai wuh.

What crops grow in this country=Pah de mulk ke sah faslúnah paida kegi.

Wheat, Barley, Maize, Mustard, Rice & Sugar Canes=Ghanam, Orbushe, Jowár, Sharsham, Wreje aw Gani.

We must go back to the village = Pakár di chih kali tah bertah lárshú.

When will the Khan come?=Khan bah kalah ráshi.

He will come, when he has done his work=Chih khpal kár wukri no rá bah shi.

EXERCISE 9.

WRITTEN.

Have you learned Pushto? I have read a book. Who has written this letter? Have you seen the country of Cabul? I have been (have gone) as far as (up to) Ali Masjid. What is the news of the Khyber? Have you heard anything? I heard nothing. A sepoy from the Khyber has come on leave, (and) he has brought a letter from my brother. My brother is a Sergeant in the Khyber Rifles. Has he sent you any news? He wrote (has written), that in Tirah a big fight has taken place among the Afridis. Do you send any message to him? I write a letter to him every week. What place is this? It is Hoti. Who is that fat man. He is the Khan of Hoti. He has a big estate and his father has built many villages and is a man of great respect and influence. Whose is this garden? It is the Khan's. What fruits grow there (in it)? Peaches, Pears, Plums, Pomegranates, and Grapes and the water flows through it. Let us go (come that we may go) and have a walk in the garden. It is getting (becoming) late; we should go back home now. When will you go to the village? I shall go when I have seen the Khan Sahib,

EXERCISE 10.
ORAL.

Do you understand Hindustani ?=Tuh hinko pohegai.

Do you recognize him ?=Tuh haghah pejanai.

Ask him his name=Núm yi wupukhtah, or lah haghah nah pukhtanah wukrah chih námah di sah dah.

He says (that) his (my) name is Khwás=Haghuh wáyi chih núm mi Khawás dai.

Why have you come ?=Wale rághalai yai.

I have come to make a report=Zuh rapot kawulo dapárah rághalai yam.

What has happened ?=Sah chal shawai dai, or suh pekh shawi di.

A theft was committed last night=Begá yawah ghlá shawai dah.

Aslam's house was broken into=Da Aslam da kor kandar shawai dai.

The theives entered his house and stole a lot of property=Ghluh da haghuh pah kor ke nanawatal aw der mál yi pat kruh.

The burglary was committed from the back of the house=Kandar da kor da shá dade wushuh.

They escaped (ran away) through the gateway=Haghoe da bahar pah wruh bánde wutakhtedal.

They stabbed (struck with the knife) Aslam's son and shot two chawkidars=Haghoe da Aslam zoe pah cháruh jobal kraluh aw dwah saukidárán yi pah golo wuwajal.

A wounded thief was arrested (caught) on the spot=Yau jobal ghal pah maukah wuniwalai shuh.

A pursueing party followed them (went, or turned out after them)=Yawah chaghah war pase wuwatalah, or láráh.

I saw many robbers on the road=Má der shúkmárán pah lár bánde wulidal.

I asked them who they were? (who are you?) but they did not answer=Má tre tapos wukruh chih táso sok yá-i kho hagho ghag wu nah kruh or haghoe hes wu nah wayal aw ghali shwal.

The day before yesterday they robbed two travellers and carried off several village cattle=Ormah wraz haghoe dwah masáfar wushúka-wul aw da kali der dangar or sárwi yi botlal.

The Sub-Inspector of Police has come to make an enquiry=Thánredár sahib tahkikát lah rághalai dai.

EXERCISE 10.
WRITTEN.

Do you know (understand) Pushto ? Do you know (recognize) this man ? Ask him who he is (who are you ?). Where does he come from (or of which place are you ?). What is his name (what is your

name?) and where is he going (where are you going ?). He says, that
he is (I am) a watchman of Khazanah, his (my) name is Duránai
and he has come (I have come) to the police station to report a case.
What has occurred in the village ? A raid took place last night in
Khazanah (a raid came, or fell on Khazanah). The raiders broke
the door of a rich Hindu's house, entered and took (carried away)
cash, jewels and lots of other property. They killed a chawkidar
and severely wounded the owner of the house. A party pursued
(went after) them, but they leaving (left) the wounded soon
went off. A raider was arrested on the spot. Which is the road
to Babozái ? Will you take (lead) us ? Very well, I will lead you
to Babozái. Is the road safe or dangerous ? (Is there anything to fear
on the road or not ?) Sometimes robbers meet along the side (in
the neighbourhood) of the road. Yesterday I saw several thieves on
the road. I asked them if they were travellers (Are you travellers ?)
but they did not answer me (did not give me an answer) and ran away.
A week ago the thieves robbed some travellers and also carried
off many cattle. Who is that horseman (what is) coming ? He
is the Inspector of Police. He is going to the spot to make an
enquiry.

---o---

EXERCISE 11.

ORAL.

Young man! are you a Pathan ?=Ai zwánah tuh pukhtún yai.

Yes Khan ! I am a Mahmundzai Pathan=Ho, khánah zuh
Mahmundzai pukhtún yam.

What is your profession? Kasab di sah dai, or suh kasab kai.

I am a cultivator = Zuh zamindár yam.

Did you ever serve ? Chare nokari di karai dah kah nah.

Yes I have served 21 years in the army = Ho má yauwisht kálah
pah fauz ke nokari karai dah.

What regiment did you serve in? Pah kume paltane ke di
nokari karai dah.

I served in the 39th. Regiment = Pah yau kam salwikhtame
Paltane ke mi nokari karai dah

Did you ever go to war? Tuh chare jang tah talai yai.

I have been (have gone) to several wars = Zuh pah dero jangúno
bánde talai yam.

I have four medals = Rá sakhah salor taghme di.

Can you speak English? Tuh Angrezi wayalai shai.

I can converse in Hindustani = Pah Hinko ke khabare atare
kawulai sham.

(Since) How long have you been learning Persian? = Tuh kalah
ráse fársi zdah kai.

(Since) Six months = Shpago miáshto ráse.

Can you swim ? Tuh lámbo wahalai shai.

I am not a good swimmer = Zuh khah lámbozan nah yam.

That man can swim across the river = Haghah sarai lah sind nah pah lámbo porewatalai shi.

In the dark I could not see you = Pah tiyáruh ke má tuh lidalai nah shwai.

Can you accompany me (go with me) up to Ali Masjid? = Tuh rásarah Ali Masjid pore tlai shai.

You can take (lead away) my comrade = Tuh zamá margarai botlai shai, or bozah.

He can take (lead away) the chawkidar with him (with himself) = Haghah di zán sarah saukidár bozi or saukidár di zán sarah kri.

EXERCISE 11.
WRITTEN.

Who are you, young man? I am an Afridi Pathan. What work do you do? I am employed (I am a servant). Where are you employed? I am employed in the 40th. Pathans regiment. How much service have you and have you ever been (have gone) on active service? I have (of) nine years service and have been (have gone) on active service in China and Mohmunds Expedition and have two medals. Were you ever wounded in War? I was slightly (little) wounded, but my cousin who was a very strong and brave soldier was killed in War. In the War how were the enemy armed (what kind of weapons had the enemies?) They were very badly armed (They had very bad weapons). Can you speak Hindustani? I cannot speak, but I can understand people speaking. My Company Officer learns Pushtu. How long has he been learning Pushtu? (Since) Three months, and in (after) six months he will be able to speak well. Can you swim across the river (Can you get across the river by swimming?) I cannot swim; my companion is a good swimmer. Last night it was so dark that I could not find the road. Can you accompany me (go with me) up to Landi Kotal? I will take (lead) you with me (with myself). You can take (lead) your (own) servant with you (with yourself). The Khan can take (lead) his man with him (with himself).

EXERCISE 12.
ORAL.

The Judge ordered his peon to go to the plaintiff and tell him to attend (or come to) the Court himself = Munsif Sahib khpal chaprási tah hukum wukar chih muddá-i tah lárshah aw wartah wuwáyah chih adálat or kachará-i tah pukhpalah ráshah.

The defendant could not attend himself, but he has sent his agent instead (in his place) = Muddaáiae pukhpalah rátlai nah shuh magar haghuh pah pukhpal záe khpal mukhtiár or wakil rálegalai dai.

I thanked God when I reached home safely = Chih kortah Sahih Salámat, or pah khair khairiat ráwurasedam no shokar mi wukar.

The robbers seized me and I saw that there was no (way of) escape = Chih shookmárano zuh wuniwalam no má wuwayal chih lár da khlásedo nishtah.

He struck me so, that I gave up hope of my life = Haghuh dáse wuwahalam chih da jwandah ná umedah shwam.

When I had climbed up the hill, I felt (understood) that I could not get down = Chih ghruh tah wukhatam no poheshwam chih kuzedai nah sham.

Did the headman strike the boy? = Malak halak wuwahalah sah.

The same man abused him = Hum haghe sari wartah kanzal wukral.

A murder has been committed = Yau khún wushuh.

Dont hurt that poor fellow = Haghah gharib or ájiz mah khúgawah.

He opressed me = Haghuh zuh tang kram.

He has come (himself) to his house = Haghah khpal kortah pukhpalah rághai.

He was a man like you = Haghah stá ghunde or stá pah shán sarai wuh.

He is as strong as a wrestler = Haghahd a pahlawán pah shán mazbút dai.

Do you know anything about this matter? = Tuh da de khabare nah sah khabar yai.

Place the carpet here, don't place the book there = Daltah lamsai wáchawah haltah kitab mah gdah.

Go out of the house = Lah korah bahar wúzah.

The Khan has sent for you = Khán tah balalai yai.

EXERCISE 12.
WRITTEN.

The Governor gave his servant an order to go to the Khan Sahib and tell him to come himself (yourself) to see him (me). The Khan could not come himself so he sent his son instead (in his place). When I reached my country safely, I thanked God that I escaped (from) death. When I was seized by the enemy, I saw that there was no way of escape now. The thieves struck me so much that I gave up hope of (I became hopeless of) life. When the boy had climbed up the tree, he felt (understood) that (I) he could not get down. The blindman fell into the pit and felt (understood) that (I) he could not climb up. Who has struck my servant? Why did he strike you? The same man whom I abused yesterday struck me. Who has killed this traveller? When was this murder committed? Don't hurt me. Dont oppress that poor fellow. Whose knife is this? It is my own. I have seen many men like you. He is as strong as a

Tiger and brave as Rustam. That man is as fat as a bull, but as foolish as an ass. The Nawab Sahib is a liberal as Hatam, and as wise as Lokman. He got up in anger and went away, saying that he (I) would never come again. Do you know (are you informed) where he is? Where have you placed my book? Don't go out of the house as it is raining. He sent me a letter saying that he (I) will come himself (myself) to see you The Magistrate has summoned (has sent for) the accused personally (himself).

————o————

EXERCISE 13.

ORAL.

The state of the country is very bad ▬ Da mulk hál der kharáp dai.

On account of no rain, severe drought, and famine the whole district is ruined ▬ Pah sabab da nah kedalo da bárán aw sakhte sokre aw qát tolah alákah (or tapah) wránah shwah.

All villages are deserted, and the villagers have fled to well favoured countries = Tol kali wrán shwal (or kháli shwal) aw kaliwál abádo mulkúno tah wutakhtedal.

The irrigated and unirrigated lands are both lying waste = Awi aw lalmi dwárah zmake sháre prate di.

There is no sign of greenness in the country = Pah mulk ke da shin boti nakhah nishtah.

Owing to plentiful rains in the plains the country is well favoured by nature. Pah samo ke da der báránúno pah sabab mulk khah abád dai.

The Cabul River is in flood, all the fields are over flowing with water, and the ponds are full to the top ▬ Pah landi sind ke silábr ághalai dai, tol pati da abo nah dak di aw dandúnah sar tar sarah dak di.

The farmers began to plough and sow their lands = Zamidarán pah khapalo zmako yawe kawulo (or arawulo) aw karalo (or pah kar) lagyá shwal (or akhta shwal).

The Government gives them help in money for cultivating purposes ▬ Sarkár wartah zamidári (or kar) dapárah taqáwi warkawi.

The red and white corn, or the summer and winter crops will both be grown well this year = Srah aw spinah ghalah (grain), yá da da aori aw da mani dwárah faslúnah sagkál bah khah wushi.

In hot countries, the wheat has been reaped, and harvested = Pah tod (or garam) mulkúno ke ghanam lao shawi (or rebali shawi) di aw ghobal shawi di.

Peaches are in season and are ripe, but pomegranates are not in season and are yet unripe = Da shaftáláno wakht dai aw pákhuh di kho da ánáro wakht nah dai aw lá kachah di.

EXERCISE 13.
WRITTEN.

The state of the country is now much better than it was before. The scarcity of rain in the last three or four years greatly ruined the country. Owing to the severe drought and famine most of the villages were deserted and the people fled to well favoured countries. Not only the lands depending on the rain, but the lands under canals and Persian wheels were also lying waste. The irrigating channels and the wells were dried up, even the rivers had little water flowing in them. There was no sign of greenness in the country there. Now when it rained heavily this year, the country was again well populated, and is well favoured by nature. Lands, fields, plains, deserts, roads, and streets are over flowing with water. Rivers and streams are flooded, fountains, tanks and ponds are full to the brim. The people began to return to their homes. The poor farmers are busy in ploughing and sowing their lands. They are getting a great deal of help in money from the Government, therewith buying bullock teams and seeds for cultivating purposes. The winter and summer crops will flourish, the farmers will become rich, and the Government will receive a considerable amount of revenue this year. In this country the red corn such as wheat, barley, and gram is sown in the autumn, and is reaped and harvested in the summer; while the white corn such as rice, maize, and millet is planted in the spring and is reaped in the winter. Fruits are yet unripe in the gardens. Peaches, soft plums, etc.; will ripen in rains. Grapes, Apples, Pomegranates, Cabul mellons, and many dry fruits are coming from Cabul.

———o———
EXERCISE 14.
ORAL.

The Commander-in-Chief and all his troops were on manoeuvres = Sepáh Sálár sarah da khpalo lakhkaro pah julsah bánde wú.

While the foot and mounted troops were engaged in parading, and firing, they received an order from the War Minister for mobilization = Piyádah (or plo) aw swárah fauzúnah pah kwáedúno aw chánmárá-i kawulo lagyá wú, chih wazir da jang wartah hukam da jang da tayárá-i rawástáwuh (or ráwuleguh).

The troops left their stations at sunrise and reached the front in the afternoon = Fauzúnah da khpalo cháwnro nah nwar khátuh rawán shwal aw máspakhim da jang záe (or sarhad) tah wurasedal.

When the battle was began the soldiers fought bravely, advancing and repulsing the enemy's attack, and charged them fiercely with bayonets = Chih jang wunkhatuh, spáhiáno pah túrzantob sarah jang wukuh, wránde (or mukhke) kedal, da dúshman hamlah yi pah shá kawulah aw pah singinúno yih sakhtah hamlah pre wukrah.

At the first attack we retreated, but at the second one we dispersed, the enemy and completely defeated them taking position = Pah

awalah hamlah múng wrasto (or pah shá) shú, kho pah balah halah
mu dushman wutakhtawuluh (or khwáruh kral), aw loe shikast (or
mátah) mu warlah_wárkrah aw morchah (or záe) mu tre láude kar
(or wákhist).

It is said that many of the enemy were killed, wounded, and
captured = Wáyi chih der dushmánán wu–wajali (or qatal) shwal,
jobal (or zakhmián) shwal aw wuniwali shwal.

A few machine guns, much munitions, and food; supplies were
taken = Yau so pechi tope, der sámán da jang aw da rasadúno
pah lás rághlal.

Our trenches were dug in a well guarded place, and were in a safe
condition = Zamúng morche pah panáh záe ke kanastalai shawe we aw
amni ámán we.

Owing to our trained soldiers, and good munitions, such as modern
rifles, machine guns, bombs, airships, war ships, mechanical (motors)
transport and ammunition, and good arrangements of supplies, we
gained the victory = Zamúng da jang azmúdah (or hokhiár) spáhiáno pah
sabab, da khuh sáman da jang, lakah nawi topakúnah (or rapalúnah),
jangi jeházúnah Pechi tope, da bamb gole, hawá-ie (or alwatúnki)
jeházúnah motarkátúno da bárbardárá-i, aw da golo dáro aw khuh
bandúbast darasadúno mung barai biyámund.

EXERCISE 14.
WRITTEN.

The Commander-in-Chief, with his Generals, Colonels, Commanding Officers, and all the troops was on the manoeuvres. The
Infantry, and Cavalry were parading; and the Artillery were
firing; meanwhile they received an order from the War Minister
for Mobilization, so the troops began to march to their res-
pective stations (Cantonments). On reaching, they were ordered
to leave their tations at sunrise for the battle field. They marched
till they reached the front; they encamped and dug out their
trenches opposite the enemy. Next day the battle began early in the
morning. The soldiers fought bravely and advanced about six miles
repulsing the enemy. They then charged the enemy with bayonets so fiercely that they dispersed him, and caused him great
loss. On their second attack the enemy was totally defeated, and
they took his position. It is said that ten thousand of the enemy
were killed, and five hundred were captured. Twelve machine guns,
other property, and food supplies were taken. The loss on our side
was fifty officers, and five hundred men killed, and one thousand
wounded. Though the enemy's force was much larger than ours,
his position was more guarded, and his trenches being on the top of
the hill, were in a safer condition than ours which were at the foot of
the hill; yet our well trained soldiers, and good munitions such as

new rifles, machine guns, bombs, airships, warships, mechanical (motors) transport, and the best arrangements of supplies favoured us and we came off victoriously.

———o———

EXERCISE 15.
ORAL.

It is said that a certain King was very luxurious, and fond of amusements, especially of hunting, and was quite ignorant of the affairs of the country ═ Wayalai kegi chih yau bádsháh der áyásh (or ayshi) wuh, aw da sail aw da khkár der shoqin wuh, aw da mulk da maámelo nah bekhi (or bilkul) ná khabarah wuh.

The Civil and Military authorities were in the hands of a tyrant ruler who was taking bribes from the poor subjects and was careless of the internal and external state of the country ═ Da mulk aw da fauz ikhtiárúnah da yau zálim hákim pah lás ke wú chá chih bah da gharib (or ájez) rá-iyat nah bade akhistalai, aw da mulk da bahar aw da dananah da hálah nah gháfilah (or beparwá) wuh.

The first riot which occurred, was the result of mismanagement in the Civil affairs ═ Awal pasát chih úchat (or portah) shuh pah sabab da bad intezámá-i da mulki maámeláto wuh.

All Judges, Court officials, Pleaders, and Petition writers disobeyed the law by taking money unlawfully ═ Tolo qáziáno (or munsifáno), da adálat ahlekáráno, wakiláno, aw arzi nawisáno da harámo rupo da akhistelo pah sabab qánún rúd (or kharáp) kruh.

There was no justice. A good but poor man would be robbed in every way, and a wealthy but guilty man would be kept from the severities of law ═ Insáf (or adal) nah wuh, khuh kho gharib sarai bah lút keduh (or shúkeduh) aw mujrim kho daulatmand bah da qánún da sakhto nah sátalai shuh.

On account of many crimes being committed, such as murders, raids, elopement with women, adulteries and gambling a conspiracy is made in the country ═ Pah sabab da kedalo da dero jormúno lakah khununah, dáre, mateze, zinágáne aw jowáriyáne pah mulk ke pasát (or balwa, or ghadar) paidá shuh.

The outcome of all this was that the Governors could not suppress the mutiny which followed ═ Da de tole khabare anjám (or akhir or natijah) dá wuh chih hákimáno dá balwah (or ghadar or pasát) chih úchatah shwah lare (or dafah) kawule nah shwah.

Alam Khan found a good opportunity. Having collected a large force, he invaded the weak monarch's country ═ Alam Khan khah moqah biyámundah, fauz yi jamah kruh aw da kamzori bádsháh pah mulk ráwukhat.

The King's Army opposed with its utmost, but at last the Khan's army defeated them ═ Da bádsháh lakhkar pah khpal was moqábelah wukrah kho akhir ke da Khan fauz wartah shikist (or mátah) warkruh

In this war, the Prince, The Minister of War and many leaders of the army were killed ; and the King with the Crown Prince was besieged = Pah de jang ke loe (or mashar) wazir,, da jang wazir ao der da. fauz masharán (or sardárán) wuwajali shwal, ao bádsháh sarah da wali ahdah gair (or ráhisár) shah.

The Khan's army bombarded and set fire to the town = Da Khan fauz pah khár golah bári wukrah ao aor yi warpore kar.

It is stated that the khan took the capital and captured the King with his Prihce = Wayalai kegi chih khan páyetakht wákhist ao bádsháh yi sarah da shahzàdah wuniwaluh.

EXERCISE 15.
WRITTEN.

It is related, that a monarch, who was very fond of luxury and loved amusements of all kinds, and who spent most of his time hunting, left the management of his country's affairs to unscrupulous ministers The Civil and Military jurisdictions were in the hands of tyrant governors, who received bribes from the King's subjects, and who were careless of the working of the interior and exterior interests of the state. The Judges, Magistrates, and others responsible for law and orders, took bribes from either parties, Accused or plaintiff; defendant or complainant; jurispondence was miscarried. A poor (but just) man would be imposed upon in every way—a rich (and in all probability guilty) man could keep himself from the severity of the laws.. Court Officials, pleaders, and petition writers had enriched themselves by obtaining money unlawfully. Such mismanagement began to make itself manifest—capital crimes were committed, bribes were taken openly; raids were made, when money and jewellry were taken and young women kidnapped, adultery and gambling were indulged in; conspiracies to assasinate the King were brewing. The first revolt which occurred in the country was caused by the non-payment and wretched ' provisioning of the army. The King was unable to suppress the mutiny nor were his Governors more effectual in controlling the mutineers, and in suppressing the notorious bands of men which roamed the country. Salar Khan, a banished adventurer of the worse type, seized this opportunity to strike a blow against the King. He collected a large force and invaded the country governed by this weak monarch. The King's army opposed him unsuccesfully.

PART II. COLLOQUIAL.

VARIOUS USEFUL TERMS.

(Note)—Besides these various useful terms, some of the noted places are also given in these columns in order to get well acquainted with the country, and acquire a wider knowledge of the language.

The country of Afghanistan.	Da Afghanistan mulk.
The country of Persia.	Da Fáras (or Ieerán) mulk.
The country of Arabia.	Da Arabo mulk.
The country of Waziristan.	Da Waziristan mulk.
The country of Baluchistan.	Da Baluchistan mulk.
The country of Cabul.	Da Kábul mulk.
The country of Tirah.	Da Tiráh mulk.
The country of Swat.	Da Swat mulk.
The country of Bajor.	Da Bájawar mulk.
The country of Bunair.	Da Bunair mulk.
The Pushtu Language.	Da Pukhto jabah.
The Persian Language.	Da Fársi jabah.
The Arabic Language.	Da Arabi jabah.
The Hindustani Language.	Da Hinko jabah
The Punjabi Language.	Da Punjábá-i jabah.
The Bilochi Language.	Da Balochi jabah.
The English Language.	Da Angrezi jabah.
The Durani Pathans.	Duráni pukhtánuh.
The Afridi Pathans.	Afridi pukhtánuh.
The Waziri tribe.	Da Waziro qoum.
The Bangash tribe.	Da Bangasho Khel.
The Biloch people.	Balochián Khalq.
The Khatak people.	Khatak Khalq.
The Mohmand people.	Mohmundán Khalq.
The Yusafzá-i people.	Yusafzi Khalq.
The Zakka Khel Afridis.	Zaka Khel Afridi.
The Adam Khel Afridis.	Adam Khel Af idi
The Kambar Khel Afridis.	Kambar Khel Afridi.
In the Kingdom of.	Pa Bádshahi ke da.
Sultan Mahmud of Ghazni.	Sultan-e Mahmúd Ghaznawi.
In the reign of.	Pah hukam ke da.
Amir Sher Ali Khan.	Amir Sher Ali Khán.
During the rule of Duranis.	Da Duráno pah hukam ke.
In the time of the Sikhs.	Da Sikáno pah wakht ke.
His Imperial Majesty.	Shahinsháh.
King George V.	Badsháh George Pinzam.
The Capital of the Empire.	Pá-e takht.
The King's audience.	Bádsháhi Darbár.
The King's Ccronation.	Da Tájposhá-i Darbár.
The Crown.	Táj; Jaghah.

To Crown	Táj pah sar ekhodal or kekhodal
Throne	Takht
To throne	Pah takht kenawul
To dethrone	Lah takhtah kúzawul
King and Emperor of India	Bádsháh Qaiser-e-Hind
Queen Empress of India	Malikah Qaisara-e-Hind
The Crown Prince	Shahzádah Wali-ahad
The Prince of Wales	Shahzáda-e Wales
A Princess	Shahzádgá-i
The King's Palace	Da Bádsháh Monrá-i
The Viceroy of India	Wazir-e-Hind
The Prime Minister	{ Loe (or mashar) Wazir Wazir-e ázam
Minister for the Interior	Mulki wazir
Minister for Foreign Affairs	Ghair (or bálá-i) Wazir
Chancellor of the Exchequer	Wazir-e Mál
The Sea Lord	{ Da jiházúno afsar Amirul bahar.
Home Secretary	Dabir-e Mulk
The Arch bishop	Lát Pádri
The Pope of Rome	Pápá-e Rum
The Cabinet	{ Bádsháhi jargah Sháhi Majlas
The Parliament	Dewán-e Khás
Staff (Officers)	Amlah; ahlekár
Officials	Munshián
Public audience	Darbár-e ám
Private audience	Darbar-e khás
An ambassador	Safir
His Majesty	Bádsháh
The Amir of Cabul	Amir da Kábul
The Governor of Kandahar	Da Kandahar Hákim
The Khan of Qlat	Da Qlát Khan
The fort of Herat	Da Hirát Qlá
The Nawab of Dir	Da Dir Nawáb
The Mihtar of Chitral	Mihtar da Chatral
The Khan of Darband	Da Darband Khan
The Country Elders	Da mulk Masharán
The tribal council	Da qaum Jargah
The tribal allowance	Da qaum Májib
The King's Empire	Da Bádsháh Báchá-i
The King's country	Da Bádsháh Mulk
The Government's country	Da Sarkár mulk
The Government's property	Sarkári mál
The Government's boundary	Da Sarkár had (or brid)
The Government's subjects	Da Sarkár ra-iyat

Foreign country	Ghair (or pradai) mulk
Dependent territory	Ra-iyat ; Da sarkar aláqah
Under the Government rule	Da sarkár da hukam da lánde
Independent territory	Ghair aláqah; yághistán
By the Government's authority	Da sarkár pah hukam
Across the border	Lah sar haddah pore; yághi mulk
Frontier	Sarhad
Frontier Province	Sarhadi aláqáh (or súbah)
North West Frontier	Sarhad-e shimáli wa maghrebi
Great Britain	Bartániah Uzmá
The British Empire	{ Da Ferangyáno Bádsháhi Da Angrezáno Báchá-i
The Republic	Jamhúri (or Jargah dar) Saltanat
The Local Government	Maqámi Sarkar
The French Empire	Da Frans Bachá-i
The Russian Empire	Da Rús Bádsháhi
The Japanese Empire	Da Jápán Bádsháhi
The Chinese Republic	Da Chean Jamhúri
The Persian Gulf	Khalij-e Fáras
The Dardanelles	Dare-dániyál
The Suez canal	Nahr-e Swiz
The Sultan of Egypt	Da Misar Sultán
The British rule	Angrezi hakúmat
The King's Army	Da Báchá lakhkar
The Royal Army	Báchahi fauz
The Goverment's Army	Sarkári fauz
The Imperial Service	Sháhi khidmat
The Government Service	Sarkári khidmat
On His Majesty's Service	Bah kár (or pah kar da) Sarkár
The Government's duty	Sarkári kár (or naukari)
The chief Pathan	Khán Sáhib
A Pathan man	Pukhtún sarai
A Pathan woman	Pukhtanah khazah
The Pathan people	Pukhtánuh khalq
The Pathans' country	Da Pukhtano mulk
The country people	{ Alam ; aúlas ; bandiyán Da mulk khalq
The country men	Mulkiyán ; wataniyán
The common people	Am khalq ; aúlas
The public	Makhlúq ; alam ; aúlas
The Khan's estate	Da Khán kháni
The Khan's followers	Da Khán mlátarán
The Khan's order	Da Khán hokam
The civil authority	{ Da mulk ikhtiyár Da mulk wák
Peshawar City	Da Pekháwar khár

The Khyber valley	Da Khyber darah
The Kohat valley	Da Kohat darah
The Swat valley	Da Swat darah
From Jamrud	Lah Jamrud nah
To Ali Masjid	Tre Ali Masjida pore
From Landi Kotal	Lah Landi Kotal nah
To Jalalabad	Tre Jalálábáda pore
The Khyber Pass	Da Khyber Ghákhai
The Malakand Pass	Da Malakand Ghákhai
The Chakdarah Camp	Da Chakdare Paráo
The Attack fort	Da Attak qlá
The Shabkadr fort	Da Shabqadar qlá
The Drosh fort	Da Drosh qlá
The Peshawar fort	Da Pekháwar Bálá hissár
From Quetta	Lah Kote nah
To Chitral	Tre Chatrála pore
The Peshawar District	Da Pakháwar zilah
The Kohat District	Da Kohát zilah
The Nowshera Tahsil	Da Nokhár Tahsil
The Mardan Sub-Division	Da Mardan aláqah
The Hashtnagar under-district	Da Hashtnagar tapah
Camp Abázá-i	Da Abázo paráo
Camp Rustam	Da Rustam paráo
The Yusafzá-i's country part	Da Yusafzo tapah
The Khatak's country part	Da Khatako aláqah
The Bunair Sub-Division	Da Bunair aláqah
The Derajat Sub-Division	Da Derajáto aláqah
Asia	Asiyá-e Kallan
Asia Minor	Asiyá-e Kúchak
The King's regulation	Bádcháhi qánún / Bádsháhi qá-edah
The Army regulation	Fauzi á-ien / Lukhkari qánún
The Civil regulation	Mulki qánún
The Government Law	Sarkari qánún
The Mohammadan Law	Shari-at
The Hindu Law	Da Hinduwáno Dharam Shástar
The country law	Da Mulk qá-edah / Da Mulk rawáj / Da Mulk lár
The Pathans' custom	Da Pukhtano dustur / Da Pukhtano pukhto

USEFUL PHRASES.

Great God	Loe Khudá-e
Holy God	Pák Khudá-e
God's creation	Da Khudá-e paidawakht
Human being	Bandah
Human race	Bani ádam
The Universe	Jihán
To this world	De dunivá tah
In the next world	{ Pah qivámat ke Pah akhirat ke
On the land	Pah zmakah bánde
From the sky	Lah asmán nah
A high mountain (Hill)	Uchat Ghar
A low hillock	Khkatah Ghundá-i
The great sea	{ Loe Qahr-e daryáb Loe Samandar
A small river	Warúkai Sind
A large island	{ Loeah jazirah Loe tápú
A small lake	Waruke jabah
A thick forest	Ganr zangal
A tall tree	Lwarah (or Haskah) wanah
A broad plain	Plan Medán
An open place (plain)	Pránastai dág
A narrow road	Tangah lár
The hot sun	Tod nwar
The bright moon	Rokhánah spogmá-i
A shining star	Rokhánah storai
The cold water	Yakhe obuh
The hot fire	Tod aor
The dry earth	Wuchah Kháwrah
The wet ground	Lwandah zmakah
A round stone	Ghund Kánrai
A flat slab	Planah tabuá-i
A damp sand	Niyamdárah (or ziyamnákah) Shagah
A dim or foggy	Doond ; Dúndukár
The dense clouds	Gúra waryaz
The blazing lightening	Zaledunkai tandar
The light day	Ronrá wraz
The dark night	Torah shpah
An open place	Art (or pránastai) záe
A close place	Band záe
The pleasant (agreeable) breeze (air).	Khah Hawá
The contrary wind	Mukhálif bád

The favourable wind	Mowáfiqah hawá
A long road	Loeah lár
A short road	Lundah lár
A good place	Khuh záe
A bad place	Nákárah (or kharáp) áee
A fertile country	Mor mulk
A miserable country	Khwár mulk
A populous city	Abád (or wadán) khár
A ruined village	Wián (or újár) kalai
A small hamlet	Warah bándah
A big house	Loe Kor
A little hut	Warkote júngarah
A large inn	Loeah Srá-e
A good guest house	Khah Hújrah
A beautiful bungalow	Khkole Banglah
A well built house	Hawelá-i
A great man	Loe Sarai
An ordinary man	{ Warukai Sarai { Mámúli Sarai
The man of influence	{ Makháwriz Sarai { Barakati Sarai
A gentleman	Spinrobai (or ashráf) Sarai
A gentlewoman	Spinrobe (ashráfah, or nek bakhtah) Khazah
A man of the Khan's family	Khánawádah; Khánzádah
A Khan's descendent	Khán Khel
The man of good reputation	Nek náma Sarai
The man of bad reputation	Bad náma Sarai
The man of high rank	{ Khánadáni Sarai { Da loe Kor
The man of low rank	{ Kam asal (or Kamzátai) Sarai { Da Waroki Kor Sarai
A respectable man	{ Izzatdára Sarai (1) { Drúnd Sarai
A dishonorable man	{ Be izzata Sarai { Spak Sarai
The man of dignity	Da martabe kháwand
The man of good name	Nek náma Sarai
The man of bad name	Bad náma Sarai
A generous Khan	Sakhi Khán
A well known bread giver	Dodi már
A miser	Shúm Sarai; Bakhil Sarai
A charitable man	Faizrasána (or Da Khair) Sarai
An uncharitable priest	Be faiza (or Be khaira) múlá

(1) The last "a" in Izzatdára is too much, which is added for euphony; this final additional "a" is often added to a substantive, etc. for the sake of euphony and better sound.

A broad minded man	Loe zruh Sarai
A narrow-minded man	Tang zruh Sarai
A merciful man	Zruh (Tarasnák) swúnkai Sarai
A merciless person	Be tarsa Sarai
A proud master	Kabarjan málik (or ná-ik or khá-wand)
A man without pride	Be kabra ájaz (or gharib)
A poor fellow	} Kaminah Sarai
A man of low birth	}
A jealous person	Kinah gar Sarai
A man of good temper	{ Khuh zruh Sarai
	Nek niyata Sarai
A man of bad temper	{ Bad zruh Sarai
	Bad niyata Sarai
A cheerful man	Khandá makhai Sarai
A man of good nature	Khuh (or nek) Khuiah Sarai
A man of ill-nature	Bad (or Kháráp) Khúiah Sarai
A happy man	Khushála Sarai
A dejected woman	Khapah Khazah
A well-behaved man	Nek chalana Sarai
An ill-behaved man	Bad chalana Sarai
An unstable man	Hargajah Sarai
A rich merchant	Mor (or Daulatmand) Saudágar
A penniless gambler	Muflis, (or lundar) Jowáragar
A wealthy land lord	Duniyá dár ná-ik
A poor peasant	Khwár (gharib) Deqán
A respectful father	Adabnák plár
A disrespectful son	Be adabah zoe
A clever enemy	Hokhiyár dukhman
A foolish friend	Kamaqal (or nadána) áshná
The good parents	Khuh or Khwáguh mor plár
A kind friend	Mihrabánah dost
A beloved son	Khog zoe
A darling daughter	Niázbinah lúr
A well-bred man	Haláli (or asil) Sarai
An ill-bred man	Harámi (or Kam asal) Sarai
A needy Pathan	Mutázah pukhtún
An avaricious begger	Herasnák faqir
A greedy fellow	Gaidawar (or tamagar) Sarai
A patient fellow	Sabarnák Sarai
An impatient boy	Be sabra halak
A careful servant	Khabardára or paham kawúnkai) nokar.
A careless fellow	Be parwá (or Be pahma) Sarai
A simple villager	Sádah kali wál
A cunning townsman	Cháláka kháhrai
An expert mason	Ustakár (or Hunarmand) gilkár

A waster	Khushai sarai
An unskilled worksman	Be húnara ustakár
A useful thing	Da kár siz ; Da khe shai
A useless (worthless) thing	Be kára shai; Be khe siz
Quite useless	Hes da khe nah
A brave soldier	Túrzan (or Bahádur) Spáhi
A cowardly servant	Be zruh nokar
A kind officer	Mihrabána afsar
An unkind master	Ná-mihrabána ná-ik
A just ruler	Adil (or munsif) Hákim
An unjust judge	Be adla (or Be insáfa) munsif
A quiet man	Qalára (ghalai) sarai
A quarrelsome woman	Jangyálá-i khazah
A mischevious outlaw	Pasáti badmásh
A ruthless man	Ná kára sarai
A traitor ; treacherous	Farebi ; makkár
A time server	Da wakht zoe ; zamána sáz
An acquainted fellow	Balad sarai
Unacquainted	Ná balad ; ná áshná
A trustworthy man	Amánatgar sarai
An untrustworthy fellow	Khiyánatgar sarai
A tyrant ; cruel owner	Zálim (sakhtan) kháwand
A trustworthy servant	Itbári nokar
An untrustworthy servant	Be itbára (or ná itbára) nokar
A painstaking labourer	Khwári kakh mazdúr
A lazy workman	Nárást (sast) mazdúr
An insolent boy	Be adabá halak
A silly boy	Sádah halak
A selfish man	Gharazi (matlabi) sarai
A slanderer ; back biter	Chúghli khor
A quick-witted pupil	Zirak (Házir jawába) shágard
A furious person	Tund sarai
A reliable agent	Itbári gumáshtah
A rogue	Wran kárai
A ridiculous fellow	Be tamiza sarai
A sober ; (Pious) man	Parhezgár (nek) sarai
A lewd woman	Badkárah khazah
A naughty girl	Bakhilah jiná-i
A playful boy	Lobghárai halak
A wanderer	Garzedúnkai
A wasteful youth	Barbádi zalmai
A wrathful mad	Ghazabnák lewanai
A peaceful man	Be qahra sarai
An angry fellow	Qahrjan sarai
An obstinate fellow	Žadnák sarai
A lewd (lecher) person	Kásir (kanjribáz) sarai
A licentious youth	Lúchah (Badkára) zalmai

A lavish man	Barbádi ; fazúl kharsa sarai
Economist	Kam kharsa sarai
A rustic fellow	Bándesa sarai
A wild man	Zangali sarai
A thick-headed fellow	Kharmaghzá sarai
A clumsy woman	Be salúkah khazah
A far-sighted man	Andekhnák sarai
A rascal (rogue)	Múrdár (badzátai) sarai
A lunatic (idiot)	Saudá-ie sarai
A harmless snake	Be zarara már
A dangerous enemy	Zararnák dúkhman
A meek person	Tarasnák (laram) sarai
A lover	Ashiq ; yár
A love-sick man	Da ishq ranzúr sarai
A sweet-heart (f)	Máshúqah ; yárah
A procurer (woman)	Kútrain ; dalálah
A procurer (man)	Barwá ; dalál
A luxurious nawab	Aaishpasanda nawáb
A blockade	Kamaqal ; jáhil
A negro	Habshi
A boaster	Láfmár
A childlike fellow	Halak tabah sarai
A gay (cheerful) man	Khush tabah sarai
A hard-hearted tyrant	Sakht zruh zálim
A soft hearted man	Naram zruh sarai
A praisworthy person	Da sifat (stá-elo) lá-iq sarai
A sensual youth	Kásir (mast) zalmai
A well-wisher	Nek khwá ; khair khwá
An ill-wisher	Bad khwá
The loyal subjects	Nimak halál ra iyat
A disloyal servant	Nimak murdára nokar
A faithful dog	Wafádár spai
A faithless friend	Be wafá áshná
A frightened eunich	Yarandúkai (be zruh) hijrá
A fearless wrestler	Be yare (zruh war) pahláwan
An old weak man	Kamzorai (za-eef) búdá
A strong young man	Mazbút (takra zwán
A healthy person	Tundrast (jor or rogh) sarai
An unhealthy woman	Nájora (nárogha) khazah
A thing in good order	Rogh (jor) siz
A thing in bad condition	Kharáp (nákára) shai
An unbroken cup	Sábat kandaul
A smashed cup	Mátah piyálá-i
An experienced doctor	Tajrebah kár dáktar
An unexperienced physician	Ná tajrebah kár tabib
A busy writer	Ná wúzgára (lagyá) likúnkai

A dis-engaged clerk	Wúzgár Bábú
A strict governor	Zábeta (da zábete) Hákim
A lax magistrate	Be zábte majistrat
A favourable friend	Leházdára áshná
An unfavourable man	Be leháza sarai
A modest slave girl	Hayánákah (sharamnákah) winzah
An immodest slave	Be hayá (be sharma be ghairatah) mra·ai
A modest girl	Hayánákah (ghairatnakah, jiná-i
A truthful man	Rikhtinai sarai
An untruthful boy	Daroghjan halak
A straight-forward man	Sam (sáf) sarai
A swindler	Dokah báz (tag) sarai
A deceitful man	Tag sarai
A trickster	Chalbáz
A watchful sentry	Bedár pahrawál
A neglectful watchman	Gháfilá saukidár
Hard work	Sakht kár
An easy job	Asán laram) kár
An honest banker	Amánatgar (imándára) khazánchi
A dishonest servant	Be itbára nokar
An obedient son	Farmánbardára zoe
A disobedient boy	Náfarmána halak
A civilized person	Tamizdára sarai
An uncivilized man	Be tamizá sarai
A sympathetic man	Da khúgo; (nek khwá) sarai
An unsympathetic fellow	Be khúgo (bád khwá) sarai
A leader	Da sar sarai
A councellor	Maslahati
A smart man	Chábak sarai
An idle lad	Nárást (nákára halakai
A good friend	Khog (khah) áshná
A bitter enemy	Da sar dukhman
A dear companion	Khog margarai
A virtuous woman	Nek bakhtah (pák lamane) khazah
An adulter	Ziná kár (kásir) sarai
A grateful servant	Shukargúzára nokar
An unthankful slave	Ná shukra mra-ai
A grateful friend	Ehsánmand áshná
A brutal fellow	Zanáwar; Hewán
A base-born (bastard)	Harámzádah; Harámi
A lion hearted (man)	Mard; zruhwar
A weak hearted (woman)	Ná mard; be zruh; khazolai
The man of courage	Himatnák sarai
A cowardly man	Be himata sarai
A desperate fellow	Be báka sarai
A dreadful man	Haibatnák sarai

A hopeful young man	A umedwára zwán
A hopeless girl	Ná aumedah jiná i
An awkard person	Be zistah sarai
A well-dressed person	Khosh libása sarai
An ill-dressed person	Bad libása khazah
A filthy woman	Púwárah khazah
A man of absolute power	Khudsara sarai
A powerful man	Da (zor) was sarai
A weak man	Be (zora) wasá sarai
A certain (doubtless) thing	Be shube siz
A doubtful thing	Shubah nák shai
A devil (satan)	Shetán
A devilish act	Shetáni kár
A noble (without pride) man	Be krake (loe) sarai
A hateful woman	K:akjanah khazah
The present man	Házir or (maujúd) sarai
An absent boy	Ghair házir halak
A deserter	Takhtedúnkai or farári
A successful man	Murádmand (maqsúdmand sarai
An unsuccessful man	Ná muráda sarai
A tired farmer	Starai (stománah) zamidár
A countryman	Watani (mulki) sarai
A neighbourer	Gwándi
An excited fellow	Wár khatá ; aotar
A chatterer	Dopemár ; khabarlose
An able (worthy) man	Qábil (lá-iq) sarai
An unworthy man	Ná qábila ná lá-iqa) sarai
A jolly person	Da mazai sarai
A wicked dog	Bad spai
A wicked fellow	Bad sarai
Fond of (keen on) shooting	Da khkár shoqin or shoqi
Not fond of ; not keen on	Be shoqá
An aggressor	Da pasád jarah
An agreeable man	Rázi (khushála) sarai
A disagreeable man	Ná ráza (khapah) sarai
A pleasant thing	Khwakh shai
Agreed ; accepted	Manalai ; qabúl karai
Disagreed ; unaccepted	Námanali ; náqabúlá
Sanctioned or granted	Manzúr ; qabúl
Unsanctioned (not sanctioned)	Ná manzúr ; náqabúla
Ready; perpared	Táyár
Not ready	Ná tayár ; tayár nah
Employed ; engaged	Nokar ; logyá ; pah kár bánde
Unemployed ; disengaged	Be kára ; be nokará
The required thing	Pah kár shai
Unrequired	Pah kár nah

An urgent order	Zarúri hokam
An ordinary order	Mámúli hokam
Alive man	Jondai sarai
A dead man	Mur sarai
A sick soldier	Nájora (nárogha) spáhí
A wounded thief	Jobal (zakhmi) ghal
The man (was) shot dead	Pah golá-i mur sarai
A murdered man	Wajalai shawai (qatal shawai) (maqtúl) sarai
A murderer	Khúni ; qátil
An acquitted prisoner	Rahá (khlás) shawai qaidí or bandi
An arrested criminal	Niwalai (griftára) mujrim
A prisoner	Qaidi ; bandi
An imprisoned person	Hawáláti ; bandi
A mounted man	Sor Sarai
A dismounted soldier	Plai (pah khpalo khpo) spáhí
An astonished officer	Hairán afsar
A free man	Azád sarai
An exempted man	Khlás (ma-áf ; bakhalai) sarai
A Favourite food	Da maze (da khwand ; khwand-nákahor khah) doda-i
Tastless food	Be maze (or be khwanda) dodá-i
A fruitful tree	Mewah dára (bar dára) wanah
A fruitless tree	Be mewe (be bara) wanah
The dark shade	Ganr sorai
The light shade	Rangai sorai
A childless woman	Búra khazah
A childless man	Mirát sarai
A heirless man	Lá warisa (mirát) sarai
A barren woman	Shundah khazah
A sterile man	Shund sarai
A confined (pergnent) woman	Umaidwárah khazah
A calving cow	Blárbah ghwá
A heavy load	Drund bár
A light boundle	Spak pand
A loud noise	Pah zora (ghag ; nárah) shor
A low voice	Wro awáz
A populated place	Abád (wadán) zá-e
A disolated place	Wrán (aújár) zá-e
An educated man	Ilam dára (lwastúnkai likunkai) sarai
A beginner (learner)	Mubtadi ; nawai
An uneducated man	Be ilma sarai
An illiterate man	Ami (jáhil) sarai
An ungodly worker	Gumráh (jáhil) mazdúr
A good comrade	Khuh mal or margarai

A bad companian	Nákára margarai
A man sitting seated)	Nást sarai
A man standing	Walár sarai
A man sleeping	Auduh sarai
A man awaking	Wikh sarai
A man waiting	Hisár sarai
A Mohammedan	Músalmán
An infidel	Káfir
A far place	Lare zá-e
A near place	Nizdai zá-e
A straight road	Neghah (samah) lár
A crooked road	} Kagah wagah lár
A zigzaz road	
A safe road	Be yare (be khatare) lár
A dangerous road	Da yare (khatarnákah) lár
A narrow road	Tangah lár
A broad road	Planah (artah) lár
A hasty fellow	Talwárjanai sarai
A Quick man	Garandai (jald báz) sarai
A slow man	Wro sarai
A victorious army	Barainák (war; fatehmand) fauz
A defeated army	Mátah khwarale (par) lakhkar
A hungry man	Wugai sarai
A satisfied (fed or full) man	Mor sarai
A thirsty man	Tagai sarai
Swift water	Garandá-i (teze) obuh
Running water	Rawáne (behedúnke) obuh
Still water	Waláre (qaláre) obuh
A full pitcher	Dak mongai
An empty cup	Tash or kháli kandoal
An old man	Zor (spingeerai; búdá) sarai
An old woman	Zarah (spinsare; búdá-i) khazah
A middle-aged man	Nimzálai sarai
A middle aged woman	Nimzále khazah
An aged man	Aúmar khwaralai sarai
A damsel	Peghlah jiná-i
A handsome lady	Khá-istah (pair makhe) bibi
An ugly lass	Bad rangah (bad shikle) jiná-i
A tall husband	Dang sakhtan
A short wife	Madrá-i (jakah) khazah
A wretched widow	Bad nasibe (bad bakhtah) kundah
A sorrowful orphan	Ghamjan yateem
A happy mistress	Khushálah mairman
A dejected maid	Khapah nokarah

A lucky man	{ Bakhtawar; da bakht kháwand; Da nasib kháwand; qismatnák.
A lucky woman	{ Bakhtawarah; da bakhtmerman; Da nasib merman; qismatnákah.
An unlucky fellow	Bad bakhta; bad nasibah; badqismatah
A baby	Masúm
A young man	Zwán sarai
A young youth	Zwán zalmai
A good looking man	Daul dára (pah shikal khuh) sarai
A poor looking fellow	Be daula (pah shikal nákára) sarai
A bride-groom	Zalmai; halak
A beautiful bride	Khkole náwe
A bride's maid	Sahelá-i
A married man	Wáduh karai sarai
A bachelor	Lwand; zalmai
An unmarried man	Ná wáduh karai sarai
A betrothed girl	Kuzhdan karai janá-i
A family man	Tabardár (áyáldára) sarai
A stout youth	Chobar zalmai
A shrewd lad	Poh-e halakai
An ignorant (girl) lass	Ná poh-ah jiná-i
A swift horse	Garandai (tez) as
A slow mare	Wro (matah) aspah
A quiet horse	Asil as
A vicious horse	mast as
A lame ass	Gud khar
A crippled man	Shal sarai
A blind man	Rúnd sarai
A one-eyed boy	Kánrai halak
A blue-eyed man	Shin stargai sarai
A squint (cross) eyed man	Chaghar sarai
A clear sighted man	Nazarbáz sarai
A deaf man	Kúnr sarai
A stone blind man	Pah tapo rúnd sarai
A dumb boy	Gúngai halak
The dumb animal	Be zubánah zanáwar
A bald man	Ganjai sarai
A stuttering boy	Chárá halak
A fair boy	Spin poste halak
A woman of dark complexion	Tor bakhane (skánrah) khazah
A flat-nosed man	Cheet poze sarai
A man with mumps	Da ghur (ghurai) sarai
A dark girl	Torangrá-i jiná-i
A white-spoted man	Bragai sarai
A man without front teeth	Kandáwai sarai

A one handed (or earless) man	Búrai sarai
A pitted (marked) face boy	Teepe teepe makhe halak
A tailless bullock	Be laká-i (búrai) ghwaai
A hunch-back	Kobai
A dark man	Tor sarai
A brown man	Ghanam rangai sarai
Red colour	Súr rang
Reddish colour	Súr bakhan
Black dog	Tor spai
Blackish	Tor bakhan
A white cloth	Spin zarúkai
A whitish colour	Spin bakhan rang
A yellow flower	Ziyar gul
A yellowish colour	Ziyar bakhanai rang
A grey dog	Brag spai
Brown paper	Bádámi kághaz
Blue sheets	Khur Sádarrúnah
Blueish colour	Khar bakhanai rang
Green grass	Shin wákhuh
Pink rose	Zarghún (sosan) gul
The cheap (wares) things	Arzánah saudá
The expensive (wares) article	Gránah saudá
A cheap jack ; cheap seller	Arzán poshai
A dear seller	Grán poshai
A stout man	Sorab (ghat) sarai
A thin woman	Khwárah (nará-i) khazah
A fat bull	Sorab sandá
A scraggy buffalo	Khwárah mekhah
Sweet fruit	Khwagah mewah
Bitter poison	Trikh zahar
Saltish meat	Traskoonah ghwakhah
Brackish (saltish) water	Málgine (khora or Tarwe) obuh
Sour pickless	Triw achár
Inspid taste	Pikah (mazah) khwand
Good taste	Khuh (da maze) khwand
A fresh loaf	Tázah dodá-i
Stale bread	Sarah dodá-i
Stale fruit	Da dero wrazo (zarah) mewah
A rotten egg	Skhá agá-i or há
Thick milk	Teeng pá-i or shoduh
Thin milk	Naram pá-i
A sharp sword	Terah túrah
A blunt knife	Pasah cháruh
A coarse cloth	Ghat zarúkai
A fine cloth	Mohinah jámah
A profitable job	Súd mand (fá-edah mand) kár

An unprofitable work	Be sùda or be fá-ede kár
A great loss	Sakht or loe ziyán or nuqsán
A new rifle	Nawai topak or rapal
A old gun	Zor topak
A clean place	Pák (or sáf or sútra) zá-e
A dirty place	Khachan (or nápáka or paleet) zá-e
A rusty sword	Zang wahale tùrah
A valuable pearl	Da dere ba-ye (qimat bahá) marghalarah
An inexpensive jewel	Da lage ba-ye (kam qimata) kálai
A relative	Khpal ; khpalwán
A foreigner ; stranger	Pradai ; ghair or baharanai
Stolen property	Da ghlá mál
An eloping lover	Matizah khazah
An elder brother	Mashar wror
A younger son	Kashar zoe
A second sister	Meanzná-i khor
A youngest daughter	Lah tolo nah warkote lúr
A drunken man	Sharábi sarai
A gambler	Jawárgar
A smoker	Chilam khor
An opium eater	Afimi
A quail fighter	Batair báz
A boy lover (he who loves boys)	Bache báz
A bhang drinker	Bhangi
A snuff taker	Naswári
A chars smoker	Charsi
A madak smoker	Madaki
A man drunk	Pah nashah ke sarai
A senseless man	Be khodah (or be hosha) sarai
A sensible man	Pah khod (hosh) ke sarai
A mad man	Lewanai sarai
A pet cat	Sátale (pálale) pisho
A domestic hen	Koraná-i chargah
An adopted boy	Pálalai halak
About ten men	Takhminan las sari
Concerning him	Da haghah pah báb (bábat) ke
Above the head	Da sár dapásah
According to order	Pah Mojab da hukam
In future	Pas lah de ; pas tah
After a month	Yawe miyáshte pas
Behind the regiment	Paltane pase or paltane nak wrasto
Afterwards	Pas tah ; wrasto
After a little while	Lag sá-at (mál) pas
After a long time (period)	Derah múda pas

The Khan alone	Yawáze khán
A lonely place	Khoshai zá e
Along with me	Rá (má) sarah
Along with you	Dar (tá) sarah
Along with him	War (haghuh) sarah
Along the road-side	Da lár pah khwá ú shá
Along the river-bank	Da sind pah ghárah
Around the country	Lah mulk nah cháperah
He also	Haghah hum
All at once	Pah you wár or dam or zal
Although the khan	Agar kah khan
They altogether	Haghoe tol tál
Alright; very good	Khah ; derah khah
Not at all	Hado nah; bekhi nan ; hergas nah
Again and again	Biyá biyá
Against me	Zama pah barkhiláf
All the people	Tol (wárah) alam or makhlúq
He always	Haghah múdám or hameshah
Among pathans	Da pakhtano pah meanz ke
Alas! the khán	Armán khán
Amongst ourselves	Zamúng pah khpalo (meanz) ke
Another one (person)	Bal sok ; bal yao
Another one (thing)	Bal yao ; bal sah
Others	Nor
Any how (anywise)	Har shán ; har rangah
Anyone else	Bal sok ; nor sok
Anything else	Bal sah ; nor sah
Anywhere	Har chartah
Anywhere else (somewhere else)	Bal chartah
As many troops as	Somrah der fouzúnah chih
As a pathan	Da pakhtún ghunde or pah shán
As long as	Tre so chih ; tre kame chih
As well as that	Haghah hum
As yet	Tre aosa ; lá
As far as	Tre kame chih
As far as this	Tre de pore
As much as	Somrah ziyát (der) chih
As far as concerned	Tre so chih ta-alaq dai
Apart from this	Lah de nah (biyal) sewá
As it is	Lakah chih dai
As it was	Lakah chih wuh
As if he was a wrestler	Lakah or gunde chih pahlawán wuh
At kabul	Pah kábal ke
At this rate	Pah de naikh
At home	Kor ; pah kor ke
At the front	Makh ke or wránde

At the rear	Wursto ; pah shá
At the back of a wall	Da dewál pah shá
At all events	Pah har hál ke
At all times	Har wakht
At any rate	Pah har (súrat) shán
At first	Pah awal ke ; awal
At length ; at the end	Pah akhir ke
At least	Kam az kam ; tar so chih
At pleasure	Pah (razá) khwakhah
On this	Pah de
On that	Pah haghe
Bad, worse, worst	Kharáp; der kharáp, la tolo kharáp
Because of this	Pah da (wajah) sabab
Large, larger, largest	Loe, der loe, lah tolo nah loe
Before this	Lah de nah (awal or wránde) pah khwá
Before me	Zamá pah makh ke or da wránde
Behind the wall	Da dewál pah shá or wrasto
Through the valley	Da dare pah meanz ke
Belongs to me	Zámá (or mi) dai
Belongs to you	Stá (or di) dai
Belongs to him	Da haghuh (or yi) dai
Besides this	Sewá (or be) lah de nah
Besides that	Be (or Sewá) lah haghe nah
Beyond the boundary	Lah bud nah pore / Lah bred nah haghah khwá / Lah hadah warhístah
Both men	Dwárah sari
But (only) one horse	Kho or wale (or magar or lekin) yao as.
By the office	Daftar sakhah / Daftar tah nizde
By all means	Zarúr ; kám ná kám ; zázarúr
By and by	Pah lag (sá-at) wakht ke
Bygone	Ter shawai
By this way	Pah de (or shán or rang) lár
By that way	Pah haghe lár (shán or rang)
By the same way	Hum pah haghah lár (or shán or rang)
By which way	Pah sah or kam (or shán or rang) lár
By the sword	Pah túrah
Carefully	Pah (khabardárá-i; bedárá-i) paham
Certainly not	Hechare (herges) nah
Carelessly	Pah be (be khabrá-i) pahamá-i
A certain man	Yao or flánkai sarai
Certainly it is so	Be shakah dáse oah

For certain	Yaqini
Direct road	Neghah (or samah) lár
During the day	Pah wraz ke ; da wraze
Each of these	Har yao da dui nah
To each man	Har sari tah ; sari pah sar
Either one	Har yao
Either of these horses	Yá dá de asúno nah
Either of those mules	Yá lah hagho khacharo nah
Either this or that	Yá dá yá haghah
Either side	Dwárah (khwá ; palao; taraf) dade
The end of it	Sar (akhir) yi
Even this	Dá hum
Everybody	Har kas ; har sok
Everything	Har (or shai) siz
Elsewhere	Bal (nor) chartah
Everywhere	Har (or zá-e) chartah
Equal to this	De sarah brábar
The endless sea	Be (hada or sara or intehá) samandar
Empty purse	Kháli (tashah) boskhaká-i
Enough money	Káfi (bas ; dere) rúpá-i
Entirely good	Be shána ; hada) khah
Evergreen plant	Mudámi shin bútai
Everlasting thing	{ Derah múda kedúnkai shai
	Da tol úmar siz
Evil act	Bad (or nákárah) kár
At the end	Pah akhri ke
Exceedingly nice	{ Be shána (be hada) da maze
	Balá da maze
Supplies etc.	Rasadúnah waghera
In exchange of it	Pah badal (zá-e) ke yi
Extra duty	Ziyátah nokari or kár
If ever	Kah chare
For ever	Hameshah dapárah
Face to face	Makhá makh
Far away from here	Lah daltah nah lare
From near	Lah nizde nah
From afar	Lah (lare) wráyah
For me	Zmá (or má) dapárah
For you	Stá (or tá) dapárah
For him	Haghuh dapárah
For her sake	Da haghe da khátera
For whom	Chá dapárah
For what	Sah dapárah ; sah lah
For them	Haghoe dapárah
From the beginning	Lah awal nah

Few men ; formerly	Yao so sari ; pakhwá or awal or wrunbai
From here ; from hither	Lah daltah nah lah hishtah nah
From where ?; from whither	Lah chartah nah ; lah chartah ná-chartah nah
For your welfare	Stá da khair (kho or súd) dapárah
For what ?; for your benefit	Sah dapárah ; stá da fá-ede (súd) dapárah
For this reason ; for their loss	Pah de (wajah) sabab ; da haghœ da ziyán dapárah
From this side, or that side	Lah de khwá nah ; yá da haghe khwá nah
From the front side, or from the rear side	Da makh ke dade nah yá la wrosto taraf nah.
From the right hand, or left hand	Lah khi lás nah yá da kinr (or gas) lás nah
From the east	Lah (mashriq) nwar khátuh nah
From the west	Lah (maghrib or qeble) nwar prewátuh nah
From the north to the west	Lah (shimál) qotab nah tar (janúb) sohail pore
Have I the rifle ?	Rá sakhah topak shtah
Had you the sword ?	Dár sakhah túrah wah
He has a son ; she had a daughter	Zœ yi shtah (or dai); lúr yi wah
Have we the horse?; had he a knife?	Rá sakhah asúnah shtah ; war sakhah cháruh wah
Had they any arms (weapons) ?	War sakhah wasle we
Here and there	Daltah (dale) ao haltah
Here is another plan	Yawah balah saláh dah
Hither and thither	Histah (de khwá) warhistah (haghah khwá
Here I am ; here you are (look or see)	Zah dá yam ; wudi lid or wákhlah or wugorah
Here it is ; where is it ?	Dá dai ; chartah (kamzá-e) dai
He is doing well	Kár yi (jor) khuh dai
He is in great affliction	Hál yi bad dai or haghah pah badah wraz dai
He is at home ; she is not at home	Haghah kor dai ; haghah kor nishtah
How many more men ?	Nor samrah (or so) sari
How nice (good) it is ?	Sangah (da maze) khuh dai
How near and how far ?	Somrah nizde ao somrah lare
How long and how broad ?	Somrah úgad ao somrah plan (or art)
How is he ?; how was she ?	Haghah sangah wuh ; haghah sah rangah wah

How is this? ; how is that ?	Dá sangah dai; haghah sah rangah wuh
How was it? ; how long since ?	Sangah ; Kalah ráse
How long ago ? however	Somrah Mùdah shawe; har rangah or shán
How many days ago ; how often ?	So wraze shawë di ; so wárah or zalah
I myself or you yourself	Zah pakhpalah yá tuh pakhpalah
Then he himself	Na haghah pakhpalah
It may be so or it may not be so	Dáse bah wi yá dáse nah bah wi
If this is the case or 'if it is so	Kah dáse (súrat) khabrah dah
If such may be the case	Kah (ma-ámelah) khabarah dáse wi
If the matter is so	Kah (moqademah) khabarah dáse dah
If such is the case.	Kah khabara dá (shán) rang dah
It is no matter	Dá hes Khabarah nah dah
Is it possible, or impossible ?	Dá kegi (mumkenah dah) kah nah kegi (ná mumkenah dah)
It is a clear case	Dá sargandah khabarah or ma-ám-elah dah
It is of no use, yes, it is of use	Dá da (kár) khe nah dai, ho dá da (fá-ede) khe dai
It is quite useless; or, it is of no use whatever ?	Dá hes da khe nah dai
Indeed it is so, no it is not so	Beshakah dáse dah, nah dáse nah dah
In front of me	Zamá da wránde (or pah makh ke)
Is it enough ? Oh yes!	Bas (káfi or der) dai; ya ho
Instead of this	Da de pah zá-e) badal ke
Inner side or in the midst of it	Dannah taraf yá pah meanz ke yi
In this way (manner)	Dá (rang) shán or dáse
In that way	Haghah (rang) shán or haghah se
In which (what) way?	Sangah or pah sah rang or shán
In any way	Har rangah or pah har shán
If so ; is it so ?	Kah dáse wi ; dáse dah sah
Is it ?; is it not ?	Dah; dah kah nah
If not (otherwise); is he ?	Kah nah wi; dai (is) or wi (exists)
Is he here, or is he there ?	Haghah daltah dai kah haltah dai
Is there any one here or not ?	Dale sok shtah kah nah
Is there any one, or anything, there?	Haltah sok yá sah siz shtah
It is said ; it has been said	Wáyi or wayalai kegi ; waylai shawi di
It is related ; it is believed	Naqal dai ; yaqin dai
I think ; I believe	Khiyál (or gumán kawam ; yaqin mi dai

In my opinion ; I am of the same opinion	Zamá pah fikar ke ; zamá hum dá khiyál dai
It is a wonderful story	Dá ajeebah qisah or qisá-i dah
Is he ever here ?	Haghah chare daltah wi
It is therefore (adviseable), befitting	De dapárah khá-i or zakah munásib di
Is that all ?; not at all !	Dá tol dai or di ; hado (hechare) nah
Is this the way ?	Dá lár dah sah
If this is the custom ?	Kah dá (lár or rawáj) dastúr dai
It is not ; is it not ?	Da nah dai ; dáse nah dah sah
It was he ; it was not me	Dá haghah wuh ; zah nah wam
Is it true ? ; no it is a lie	Rikhtiyá di, nah bekhi darogh di
Is it not true ? yes, it is quite true	Rishtiyá nah dah ; ho bilkul rikhtiyá di
If it was in my power	Kah zamá pah was ke wai
It is in your power (authority)	Stá pah ikhtiyár ke dah
It cannot be helped	Da was khabarah nah dah
It is not in his power	Haghah be wasa dai
I can't help it	Zah hes kawulai nah sham
Is it good, better or best ?	Dá khah, der (or ziyát) khah, kah lah tolo nah khah dai
It is my fault, not yours	Dá zamá (qasúr) gúnáh dah, stá nah dah
It was your mistake, not mine	Stá ghalati wah, zamá nah wah
I am very sorry ; I am very glad	Zah der (afsos) armán kawam ; zah der khushála yam
Thank you (it is kind of you)	Stá mihrabáni dah
I am highly obliged to you	Zah stá der ehsán mand yam
I obliged him	Má (pre) or warsarah ehsán wukruh
Is it bad, worse or worst ?	Dá nákára (or kharáp), der nákára, ya lah tolo nah nákárah dai
It is rather good, but could be better	Dá lagkúti khah dai, kho khuh kedai shi
Is this the same thing ?	Dá hum haghah siz (or shai) dai
Is that it ? yes in fact	Dá dai sah, ho pah asal (haqiqat) ke
Into the room ; At (in) my house	Pah kotah ke ; rá (má) karah
In (at) your house ; in (at) his house	Dar (tá) karah ; war (haghuh) karah
In the mean time	Pah de meanz ke
Just as it is ; just like this or that	Jukht dá; jukht dáse yá haghah se
Just now ; if you please	Jukht aos or pah de dam ; pah mihrabáná-i sarah jee
Last of all ; lately (recently)	Lah tolo nah wrosto ; aosanai or wrostanai

Later on ; latter one	Wrosto or pastah ; wrostanai
Lest he come	Nah bá-edub chih khán or háse nah chih khan
Less than this ; likely (probably)	Lah de nah (lagkúti) kam ; gunde or sháyad
Likewise ; level ground	Haghah se or hum haghah shán ; hawárah zmakah
Lovely home ; like this or like that	Da mine or khog kor ; dá shán yá haghah rang
Like what? ; a long time ago	Sah (shán) rang ; derah múdah shawai
Long time since ; like a fool	Derah múdah ráse ; da kamaqal ghunde (shán)
Little more ; little way further	Lagkúti nor ; lagkúti (wránde) mukh ke
Little by little ; not much	Lag lag ; der (or ziyát) nah
Many times ; many more or much more	Der (wárah) zalah ; nor der
More supplies ; merely excuses	Nor (ziyát) rasadúnah ; kháli (tashe) bháne
Moreover ; more or less	Be (má sewá) lah de nah ; kamú ziyat
Narrow pass ; nearly all	Tang ghákhai ; qariban tol
Near the fort ; No !	Qlá (tah nizde) sakhah : nah nah nah
No, never ; niether he nor she	Nah nah hechare nah ; nah haghah nah, haghe
Niether this nor that	Nah dá (or day) nah haghah
Not yet ; not at all	Lá nah ; hado (or bekhi) nah
No nobody ; no nothing	Nah hesok nah ; nah hes (siz or shai) nah
No one else ; nothing else	Bal (or nor) hesok nah ; bal (or nor) hes siz nah
Never mind	Khair dai or hes parwá (or fikar) nishtah ;
No matter ; next one	Hes khabarah nah dah ; bal yao
Neverthless ; notwithstanding	Nu hum or pah de hum ; lá hum
None ; none at all	Hes (or hesok) nah ; hado hesok (or hes) nah
Nowise ; nothing for	Hergas nah ; hes lah nah
Nowhere ; somewhere	Hechartah nah ; bal chartah
On both sides ; on this side	Pah dwáro dado ; pah de khwá
On that side ; on which side	Pah haghah taraf ; pah kam palao
On either sides ; on all sides	Pah har khawá ; pah har dadah
Occasionally'	Kalah kalah ; chare chare ; moqah pah moqah '

Offen or bequently	Aksar ; ziyát
On this account ; on account of rain	Pah de (wajah) sabab ; pah sabab da bárán
On this occasion ; once or twice	Pah de moqah ; yao zal (wár) yá dwah zalah (wárah)
One by one ; one more	Yao pah yao ; yao bal (nor)
Of course ; otherwise	Beshakah ; kah nah (wi) nu
Opposite the office	Daftar nah wránde or da daftar pah mukh ke
Ordinary one ; out of these	Yao mámúli ; lah do (dui) nah
Out of them ; outside the house	Lah hagho (baghúi) nah ; lah kora bahar
Perhaps this ; previous to this	Gunde (sháyad) dá ; pah khwá lah de nah
Previously ; plentiful, abundant	Narghúnai ; der ziyát or makhlúq balá)
Per man ; per hundred	Da sari pah sar ; salo pase
Personally	Pah khpal zán or pakhpalah
Perfectly well ; quickly	Rogh mot or jak jor sahih salámat ; zar zar
Quite good ; quite bad	Der khuh ; der (nákárah) kharàp
Quite right ; quite wrong	Bekhi (or rikhtiyá) sahih ; bekhi (da sarah) ghalat
Quite correct ; quite so	Belkul sahih ; hum dáse dah
Quite difficult ; quite easy	Der grán ; der asán
Quite ready ;	Bekhi tayár
Rather this than that	Khás dá ya haghah
Real pathan ; recent rain	Asli pukhtún ; aosanai bárán
Right you are !	Khuh wáyai or stá khabarah sahih dah
River bank ; right and wrong	Da sind ghárah ; khuh ao bad or huq ná huq
Ruined fort	Wránah (újárah) qlá
Same thing ; same time	Hum haghah siz ; hum d wakht
Since when? ; long time ago	Kala ráse ; derah múdah shawe dah
Since last year	Parusa kál ráse
Same man ; some people	Hum haghah sarai ; zine (báze) khalq
Something ; some body	Sah (shai) ; sok (sarai)
Something or other ; some one or other	Sah nah sah ; sok nah sok
Somehow ; sometime	Pah sah rang ; kalah kalah
Sometime or other, or now and then	Kalah ná kalah
Somehow or other ; somewhat	Pah sah nah sah shán ; sah qadar or lag ghunde

Somewhere ; somewhere or other	Chartah ; chartah ná chartah
Something else ; some one else	Bal (nor) sah ; bal (nor) sok
Sometime ago ; so many times	Sah múdah shawai ; domrah (wá-rah) zalah
Scarcely	Pah gránah or pah sakhtá-i sarah
Seldom	Kalah ná kalah or chare chare
Same as this ; or same as that	Da de ghunde yá da haghe ghun-de
Several men ; soon as possible	Chandá (der) sari ; sangah zar chih kegi
Such and such ; so and so	Dáse ao haghah se ; flánkai ao dingrai
Suddenly or by chance	Násápah yá nagahánah
Sure and severe punishment	Yaqini ao sakhtah sazá
Sandy ground ; separately	Shaghlore zmakah ; biyal biyal or judá judá
Side by side ; sample of it	Khwá pah khwá ; namúnah yi
Stolen property ; slowly	Da ghlá mál ; wro wro
Spare time ; stony plain	Terai or (ziyáti wakht ; kánrezai maidán (or dág)
Sufficient supplies but insufficient men	Káfi (der) rasadúnah kho lag sari
This one and that one	Day or dá yao ao haghah yau
That and the other	Dá ao haghah
That, if you ; that which	Chih kah tuh ; chih kam or kam chih
Therefore ; then	Zakah or de dapárah nu
This or that will do	Day or dá yá haghah bas (der) dai
These or those	Dúi yá haghúi
There he is or there it is	Haghah dai or á-i dai
This is of use and that is no use	Dá da (khe) kár dai ao haghah (be khe) ná kára dai
Till when? ; together	Tar kalah pore ; yao zá-e
Towards the west	Nwar prewátuh (quble) khwá tah
Towards the east	Nwar khátuh dade tah
Towards the north or the south	Qotab yá sohail taraf tah
This much or that much	Domrah (dá qadar) yá haghah homrah or haghah qadar
There about or here somewher	Haltah nizde yá daltah chartah
Thereat ; thereby	Pah de sabab (or wajah); lah haghe nah
Therefrom; therein	Lah de nah ; pah de (or haghe) ke
Thereof ; thereon or upon	Da de (haghe); pah de (or haghe)

Thereto	Haghe (or de) tah
Thenceforth ; therewithal	Pas lah haghe ; war (or haghe) sarah
Thitherward ; through	Haghah khwá ; agar kah or sarah da de
Thus to and fro	Dáse or haghah se makh ke wrosto or khkatah portah
Too little ; this one too	Der lag, day or dá yao hum
Underneath ; under the tree	Lánde or kúz or khkatah ; da wane lánde
Unless or until ; upon this	Tar so (haghe) chih ; pah de bánde
Upper one ; lower one	Portanai or pasanai ; khkatah-nai
Upside down	Khkatah portah or par makh or kúz pás or naskor
Upward ; unfortunately	Portah taraf ; pah bad bakhtá-i or bad qismatá-i
Usual thing or usually	Mámuli shai yá ám or aksar
Up to the next camp ; up till now	Tar bal paráo pore ; tar aosa pore
Very good or very well !	Dera khah dah
Was the sahib there?	Sahib haltah wuh
Was she?, wasn't he?	Haghah wah ; haghah nah wuh
Was it so? wasn't it?	Dáse wah ; nah wah sah
Was it you? it wasn't me	Dá tah wai ; dá zah nah wam
Who was it then?	Nu sok wuh
What thing? what you mean?	Sah shai ; sah di matlab dai
What for? whatever	Sah lah or sah dapárah ; har sah chih
What has been has been	Sah chih wushú haghah wushú Sah chih shawi di haghah shawi di
When? whenever	Kalan ; kalah chih or har kalak chih
Whensover ; whence	Lah kam zá-e nah ; pah sah sabab
Where? ; whereas	Chartah ; pah de or chartah chih
Whereat ; whereby	Pah (de) kam chih ; lah kam nah or pah dá
Wherefore; wherein	Kam (or sah) dapárah chih ; pah kam (yao) ke
Whereof ; whereupon	Da (chá) kam ; pah (de) kam or
Wherever; wherewith	Chartah (kam zá-e) chih ; kam (or chá) sarah chih

Whether ; why	Har or kam yao chih ; wale or sah lah
Why not ; why is this?	Wale nah ; dá wale
Why so? why is that?	Dáse wale ; haghah wale
Why is he not here?	Haghah daltah (or dale) wale nishtah
Which one? which man	Kam yao ; kam sarai
While ; who?	Tar so chih or tar haghe chih ; sok
Whose horse? to whom?	Da chá as ; chá tah
Whoever ; withhold	Har sok or sok chih ; bandúbast
Within a week	Júmah ke dananah dananah
Without him	Be (sewá or baghair) lah haghuh nah
Whither he thither she	Chartah chih haghah haltah haghah
Whole day long ; all the year round	Drastah wraz ; kálú sar
With me or us ; with thee or you	Rá sarah ; dar sarah
With him, he or them ;with whom ?	War sarah ; chá sarah
Who are you? who am I?	Sok yai ; sok yam (1)
What are you? what am I?	Tuh sah yai ; zah sah yam
What is he? who is he?	Haghah sah dai ; haghah sok dai
Who is she? who are we?	Sok dah ; sok yú
Who are you? who are they?	Sok yá-i ; sok di
Who is this? who is that?	Day or dá sok dai ; dá sok dai
Whose is this? whose was that	Dá da chá dai ; haghah da chá wuh
Who is here? who was there?	Daltah sok dai ; haltah sok wuh
Who was he? who was she?	Sok wuh ; sok wah
Who was it? what was it?	Dá sok wú ; dá sah wú
Whose was it? who are they?	Da chá wuh ; sok di
What are they? who is this man?	Haghoe sah di ; haghah sarai sok dai
Who is that woman? who are these men?	Haghah khazah sok dah ; dá sari sok di
Who were those boys	Haghah halakán sok wú
Well then! ; well khan sahib!	Khah nu ; khah khán sáhiba
Well miste:! ; well mistress!	Khah Sáhiba ; khah bibi sáhibe
Well please ; well dear!	Khah jee; khah ashná or (ayárah)
What kind of? where is it?	Sangah or sah rangah ; chartah (or kam zá-e) dai
Where was it? where were you?	Chartah wuh ; charta wá-i
Where was he? where was she?	Chartah wuh ; kam zá-e wah
Who is outside? who was inside?	Bahar sok di ; dananah sok wú

---

(1) The personal pronounce " tah" (thee or you) is understood, as the last personal termination of the verb is sufficient to indicate the person.

What is this? what thing is it?	Dá sah di ; sah siz dai
What was it? what is that?	Sah wú ; haghah sah di
What is the use of it?	Sah yi fá-edahdah
What is the matter? what was the matter	Sah chal dai ; sah chal wuh
What is the cause of it?	Sah yi sabab dai
What was the reason of it?	Sah yi sabab wuh
Which is the correct way?	Samah lár kamah dah
What is the best way?	Derah khah lár kamah dah
What is this for, without this?	Dá sah dapárah dai ; be lah de nah
What is the strife?	Sah jagarah (or pasát) dai
What was the row? what is there ?	Sah shor wuh ; haltah sah di
What is here? what is going on there (1)	Daltah sah di ; haltah sah kegi
What misfortune is this all?	Dá sah bad nasibi dah
What a devil this is ?	Dá sah balá dah
What good quality has he?	Pah haghah ke sah sifat (or khúbi) dah
Who else? what else?	Nor (or bal) sok; nor (or bal) sah
Willingly ; whatever be	Pah khwakhah sarah (lah qasdah ; sah chi wi
What fresh news is there?	Sah nawai or tázah khabar dai
What is your purpose?	Gharaz (or matlab) di sah dai
What is the disturbance?	Sah pasát dai
What is the quarrell about?	Sah jagarah dah
Where as ; yearly	Hál dá dai chih ; kál pah kál
Yes it is ; yes certainly	Ho dai ; ho beshakah
Yes of course ; yes khan!	Ho kah nah ; ho khán
Yes sir ; no dear friend!	Ho sáhiba ; nah yára (or ashná)
Yes my dear son	Ho zamá khogah zo-ea Ho zama da zrúh sara zoea or zigara
Yes please ; no please	Ho jee ; nah jee

---

(1) When the object of a sentence is not mentioned the verb must be put in the third person musculine plural.

(Every-day Conversation).

Short sentences

Oh God!; Oh lord!	Ai khudáya ; ai málika (1)
Oh Almighty!; Oh khan sahib!	Ai qáderą ; ai khán sáhiba (2)
Oh Pathan!; Oh pathan boy!	Ai khána ; (3) ai kháne (4)
Oh Youngman!; Oh youth!	Ai zwána ; (5) ai zalmaia
Oh friend!; Oh dear friend (a man !	Ai ashná ; ai khoga yára
Oh dear friend (a woman)!; Oh lover! (a man)	Ai khoge yáre ; ai khoga yára or áshiqah
Oh beloved son!; Oh darling daughter!	Ai khoga zo-ea ; ai niázbine lúre
Oh brother!; Oh brethern!	Ai wrora (6) ; ai wrúnro (7)
Oh sister!; Oh sisters	A khore ; (8) ai khwendo
Oh uncle (P)!, Oh aunt (p)!	Ai káká or truh (9) ; ai trore or cháchi (10)
Oh uncle (m !; Oh aunt (m)!	Ai mámá ; ai mámi
Oh father!; Oh daddy!	Ai plára ; ai dáдá
Oh mother!; Oh mamma!	Ai more ; ai bebe or ade or abá-i
Oh old man!; Oh old woman!	Ai bábá or spingeerya (11) ; ai abá-i (12)
Oh grand father!; Oh grand mother!	Ai nikuh or bábá ; ai niyá or amá-i
Oh grand mother (m)!	Ai abá-i or adde or niyá
Come here ; come hither (this way)	Daltah ráshah; hishtah ráshah
Come there ; come thither that way)	Haltah ráshah ; haghah khwá ráshah
Don't come ; don't go	Mah rázah ; muh zab (13)
Come please ; come nearer	Rázah jee ; nizde ráshah
Come in ; get in	Danannah ráshah; danannah shah
Come back soon	Zar bertah ráshah or zar ráwugarzah

(1) In talking "ai" the sign of the vocative case is often changed into "ya" as "yad plárá-o father, but howeν-r this "ai" or "ya" is generally rejected, as the last "a" added to a noun is enough to denote the vocation :—O Khan-Khána.

(2) To address a Pathan man if high standings,

(3)   ,,   an ordinary pathan man.
(4)   ,,   a pathan boy senior in age,
(5)   ,,   a man not yet old,
(6)   ,,   a man equal in age.
(7)   ,,   country-men or relegious or professional brothers,
(8)   ,,   a woman equal in age.
(9)   ,,   a man very senior in age.
(10)   ,,   a woman very senior in age.
(11)   ,,   a man with grey beard much senior in age.
(12)   ,,   a woman equal to one's mother's age.

(13) The negative Imperatives forms from the second roots of both verbs to come "Rátlal" and to go-Tlal is vulgar to use in pushtu ; they will be supplied by the aorist tense with the negative "nah" instead or "mah" as :—Don't come-Ra nah shai i-e (Thou may not come), but not mah ráshah ; Don't go ye-Lár nah shá-i· (may ye not go); but not mah lárshah.

Come to me may I come to you	Má (or rá) laráshah ; darsham
Come out	Bahar ráshah or ráwúzah
Come along with me or us	Rá sarah rázah or ráshah
Shall I come along with you?	Dar sarah darsham or darzam
Come along with him, her, or them	War sarah rázah or ráshah
Come if you want to?	Rázah kah rázai
Come if you like?	Kah di khwakhah wi nu rázah or ráshah (1)
Let him come	Pregdah chih ráshi or rali shi
Come back at the double	Pah dau ráwugarzah
Come slowly ; come later on	Wro wro rázah ; wrosto ráshah
I am coming ; does he come?	Zah rázam ; haghah rázi sah (2)
Go please ; go, get close	Zah jee ; zah nizde shah
Don't go ; get out ; get away	Mah zah ; wúzah or bahar shah ; lare shah
Go to him ; go in	War tah lárshah or warshah ; dananah zah
Go back ; go quickly	Bertah or pastanah zah; zar zarzah
Go again ; go out	Biyá zah ; bahar zah
Go off ; clear off	Zah lárshah ; zah zah
Go if you like ; don't go there	Zah kah zai ; haltah mah zah
Go along with me or us	Rásarah zah
I go along with you	Darsarah zam
Go run on ; go at the double	Zah wuzghalah ; pah dau or sah mandah zah
Go quickly; go slowly	Zar zar or jalt jalt zah; wro wro zah
May I go to them? ; let us go	Zah warsham ; rázah (or zah, chih zú (3)
He went ; I went	Haghah ; lár zah láram
He came and she went	Hagha rashai ao baghah larah

(1) "Chih" or "kah" generally follow the aorist tense.

(2) An interogative sentence is generally expressed by the voice of the speaker ; but sometimes "sah" (what) is placed at the end of a sentence to indicate interrogation; the pushtu interagative "sah" invariably corresponds with the Hindustani interrogation "kiya"; the former is placed at the end while the later at the begginning of a sentence as :—Are you coming? Tah rázai sah ; kiyá áp áte hain.

(3) The third person singular both musculine and feminine have three forms sometimes four for the past tense; as a rule it ought to be formed by suffixing "uh" for musculine singular and "ah" for feminine siugular to the infinitive of both transitive and intransitive verbs for the past tense, but besides this usual form there arc three othe forms, one of them is formed by striking off the last "al" or "ul" of the infinitive and adding 'uu" or "ah" and the other is formed from some verbs by deleting the 'lal"o' infinitive and suffixing "uh" or ah ; the fourth form is formed irregularly as:—(1) Laralul (2) Lárúh (he went (1) Rághlah (2) raghah-(she come), but Lár (he went) Rághai (he came) are irregular ones.

What are you doing? I am doing nothing	Sah ka-i ; hes nah kawam
What has happened or what has occurred?	Sah chal (pekh) shawai dai
Who is that coming?	Dá sok dai chih rázi
Who is that going?	Dá sok di chih zi
What do you say?; what he said?	Sah wáyai ; soh yi wuwayal
Has he said anything to you?	Haghuh dartah sah wayalai di kah nah
Tell me please, don't tell him	Rátah wuwáyah jee, wartah mah wáyah
Talk to me ; he spoke a few words	Rá sarah khabare wukrah; haghuh yawah khabarah wukrah
Say it again (repeat it); listen (hear)	Biya wuwáyah; wáwrah khabarah wukrah,
Can you converse in Pushtu?	Pah pukhtu ke khabare atare kawulai shai
Did you hear?, I don't hear	Tá wáwredal ; zah nah awram
Listen to me ; listen to what I say	Khabarah mi wáwrah ; zamá khabare tah ghwag kegdah or wunisah
Do you understand? I did understand	Tah pohegai ; zah poh·e shwam
I say khan!; take (obey) my word	Hishtah gorah khán ; zamá khabarah wumanah
Do you know him? he knew me	Tah yi pejanai ; zah yi pejand am
I recognized him when I saw him	Chih me wulid nu mi wupejanduh
Don't you know him? look at him	Tah yi nah pejanai ; wartah wugorah
Can you see him? see it	Tah yi lidai shai ; wu yi winah
Take it ; who took it?	Wákhlah ; chá wákhituh
Don't take it; bring it (inanimate)	Mah akhlah ; ráwrah
Did you bring it? don't bring it	Rá di wraluh ; mah ráwrah
Bring it (animate) ; don't bring	Ráwalah ; mah ráwalah
Who brought it? has he brought it ?	Chá ráwastuh ; haghah ráwastalai dai
Take it away (inanimate); don't take it away	Yao yi sah ; mah yi wrah
I took it away ; she had taken it away	Má yao wruh ; haghe warai wuh
Take it away (animate) don't take it away	Bo yi zah ; mah yi bozah
Who took the horse away	As chá botlaluh or botluh or botuh or bot

What do you want? I want nothing	Sah ghwárai ; hes nah ghwáram
who wanted it? is it required?	Chá wughukht ? pakár dai sah
It is not required	Pakár nah dai
What do you mean ?	Sah di matlab dai
Don't worry me ; don't bother him	Mah mi rubrawah ; mah yi tangawah
I like it, don't you like it?	Zama khwakh dai; tah yi nah khwakhai
He liked it	Haghuh khwakh karai dai
Have patience, wait (stand)	Sabar wukrah, udregah
Don't wait here, get up (stand up)	Dale mah hisáregah ; pásah
Sit down ; don't sit here	Kenah ; daltah mah kenah
Wait a bit ; wait outside	Lagkúti wárwukah; bahar hisár shah
I was waiting for you	Zah dartah hisár wam
He waited for you	Haghah dartah hisár shuh
Don't you wait for me	Rá tah man hisáregah
What do you require?	Sah di pakár di
Take as much as you require	Somrah chih di pákár wi wákhlah
Take away as much as you want	Somrah chih ghwárai homrah yaosah
How much do you want ?	Somrah ghwárai
Don't take so much ; take a little	Domrah mah akhalah; lag wákhlah
Bring much, take away little	Der ráwrah; lag yaosah
Bring him here, show it to me	Dale yi ráwalah ; rátah wukháyah
Show it to him, did you show us?	Wartah wukháyah ; rátah di wukháyal
I shall show it to you	Dartah bah wukháyam
Give it to me, I gave it to you	Rá krah, dar mi kruh
Give it to him or them; don't give it	War krah ; mah warkawah
I wan't to give it to you	Zah bah dar nah kram
Don't be nervous	Qahar mah kawah or mah tundegah
Don't fight ; don't quarrell	Jung mah kawah; jagarah mah kawah
Be quite or keep quite	Ghalai (or chup) shah
Don't make a noise	Shor (zwag or ghag) mah kawah
Stay here (remain here)	Dale hisár (or páte) shah
Why are you standing there ?	Dale wale hisár (walár) yai
Who are you waiting for ?	Chá tah hisár yai
What are you waiting for ?	Sah tah (or lah) hisár yai
I am waiting for you	Zah stá lár goram
Who are you looking for ?	Sok gorai
What are you looking for ?	Sah gorai
What purpose have you here ?	Daltah di sah matlab (or gharaz dai

Who are you after? what are you after?	Chá pase yai ; sah pase yai
Whom do you want?	Sah ghwɛrai
Wait, stop, halt; Stop (or cease) it	Udregah ; wudrawah
Be very careful	Der paham kawah
Be careful, take care	Khabardár shah
Attend to what I say	Khabare tah mi ghwag kegdah
Take it down ; lift it up	Kúz yi kah ; úchat (or portah) yi krah
Get up, mount or ride	Wukhejah, ya sor shah
Get down, dismount	Kúz shah
Look sharp, make haste	Zar shah, talwár (tádi) kawah
Be quick, hurry up	Jaldi kawah ; tádi kawah
Don't move ; don't shake it	Mah khwazah ; mah yi khwazawah
Don't touch it, leave it alone	Lás mah warwrah, pregdah
Hold your tongue	Zhabah di wunisah
It is therefore better for you	Zakkah tá dapárah khah dah
That cannot be	Kedai nah shi
It cannot be done	Dá kedai nah shi
Don't mention it	Mah yi yádawah
Don't mention (take) my name	Zamá núm mah akhlah
He is angry,	Haghah pah qahar dai
He got angry	Haghah pah qahar shuh
Don't answer me	Zawáb mah rákawah
I have bad luck	Qismat (bakht or nasib) mi kharáp dai
Why do you laugh?	Wale khándai
Who did you laugh at?	Chá sarah (or pore) di wukhandal
Don't talk to me	Má sarah khabare mah kawah
Go and talk to him	Zah ao warsarah khabare wukah
Who you talking to?	Chá sarah khabare kai
Speak aloud	Pah zorah zorah wáyah
Speak distinctly (seperately)	Biyal biyal wáyah
Speak clearly (plainly)	Sáf sáf wáyah
Open the door ; shut the window	War lare krah ; kirká-i pore krah
What has become of it?	Da haghe sah wushuh
Don't get confused	Wár mah khtá kawah
Don't be afraid	Mah yaregah
Don't frighten him	Mah yi yarawah
Don't you run away	Mah zghlah
Go, run on	Zah, wuzghalah
Why are you trembling?	Wale regdai
I don't care	Zah yi hes parwá nah kawam
Why are you standing here?	Daltah wale walár yai
Why are you sitting (seated) here?	Dale wale nást yai
What have you done about it?	Da haghe di sah chal wukruh

How this can be managed ?	Da de bah sah (chal) bandúbast kegi
What does it mean ?	Da de sah (má-ne) matlab dai
Mind ; mind your own bnsiness	Paham kawah ; khpal kár kawah
Beware ; be alert	Khabar shah ; bedár aosah
Call him ; give him a shout	Rá wu yi balah ; wartah awáz wukah
Don't shout to him	Wartah ná-re mah wahah
Who shouted to me ?	Chá rá tah awáz wukruh
Bother it ; turn him out	Tobah ; wu yi básah
Put it here ; where did you put it?	Dale kegdah ; chartah di ke-khod
I have put it there	Haltah mi ekhai dai
Put (pour) some water in it	Pah ke sah obuh wáchawah
At once ; don't be late	Pah yao dam ; drang mah tera-wah
Light the lamp ; put out the fire	Diwah balah kah ; aor mar kah
Higher the wick ; now lower it down	Bátá-i wúchatah kah ; aos yi khkatah kah
Bring it back quickly	Zor yi bertah ráwrah
Pull the rope ; pull it harder	Parai rákágah ; pah zorah yi rákágah
Wake up don't go to sleep	Wikh shah mah úduh kegah
Don't be lazy	Mah sustegah or nárásti mah kawah
All right, that will do	Khuh, bas kah
Hold the book	Kitáb wunisah
I know it very well	Rá tah khuh má lúm dai
Does he know it?	Wartah má lúm dai
Do you know (recognize) me?	Má pejanai
I knew (recognised) him when I saw him	Chih mi wulid nu wu mi pejand
Send the letter ; don't send him	Chitá-i wulegah haghah mah legah
Send for the khan ; don't send for it	Khan ráwubalah ; mah yi rágh-wárah
Don't chatter ;	Tar tar mah kawah
Don't speak so fast	Dase pah zor a zor a khabare mah kawah
Near the mosque	Júmá-at tah nizde or jumá-at sakhah
Opposite the guest house	Hujre tah makhá makh
Remember (bear in mind) ; recollect	Yád larah ; yad kah
Do you remember? I don't remember	Stá yád dái ; zamá nah yádegi
Don't deceive him	Mah yi tagah

Ask him (enquire of him)	Tre pukhtanah (or tapos) wu-kah
Ask him for money	Rupá-i tre wughwárah
Turn it round	Wu yi garzawah
Find out; search for it	Pukhtanah wukah; wu yi latawah
I looked for it	Wu mi latawuluh
Go and see	Zah ao wugorah
Go at the run or go at the double	Pah dau (mundah) zah
Please come in and sit inside	Dananah ráshah jee ao dananah kenah
Tell me your name	Num di rátah wukháyah
What is the cause?	Sah sabab dai
Don't run; don't run away	Mah zghalah; mah takhtah
Sit still don't forget	Ghalai kenah; mah herawah
Don't weep; don't be sad	Mah járah; khapa kegah mah
Try your best	Khpal khuh was (or sá-ie) wukah
He is a diligent man	Haghah khwár-i kakh sarai dai
I tried my best	Má khpal was khuh wukruh
Do it for me (Indef)	Má dapárah wukrah
Don't do it (continous)	Mah yi kawah
It is being done	Dá kegi (or shi) (1)
It is done	Wushuh (2)
I did it	Má wukruh
Can you do it?	Tah yi kamulai shae
He could not do it	Haghuh kawnlai nah shuh
Who has done it	Chá karai dai
Has it been done or not?	Shawai dai kah nah
I have finished it	Má khlás karai dai
Finish it now	Aos yi khlás kah
It is commenced	Rawán (or jári shoru) shuh
It will be finished soon	Zar bah khlás (or khatam) shi
Will you do it?	Tan bah yi wukrai
I will do it, when I have done my work	Zah bah yi wukram chih khpal kár wukam
I wish it would have been done	Kashke kah shawai wai
It might have been done	Shawai bah wi
Can it be done	Kedai shi
It could be done	Kedai shuh

(1) "Shi" is vulgar, it is old Pushtu used by hilly tribes now.

(2) "Wu" is never prefixed to the root "sh" of the verb 'shwal" (to be or become), when the nominative of a sentence preceeded by a noun as :—He may become (Haghah di wushi); He may become a lance corporal (Haghah di lais náik shi, but not wushi).

PART III.

English and Pushtu Vocabulary.

A.

Ability, qábiltob; liyáqat

Able, a, qábil; láiq

Able, to be, shwal (root) "sh"

About (in number) takhminan

About (concern) Pah báb ke; pah huq ke

Above, pre, da pásah ; portah; pás

Absent ghair házir

Abuse (pl. m.) kanzal

Abuse to v. t. kanzal kawul or kanzal

Accept to v. t. qablawul; manzúrawul

Ache, to, khúgedal

Across, to go, Porewatal; root, porewúz

Active chálák

Affair n. khabarah; ma-ámelah

Afraid, to be, yaredal

After, prep, Pas

Afternoon nmáspakhin

Again. biyá; dúbárah

Age umar

Ago, kegi; shawai dai

Air bád; hawá

Alive jwandai

All tol; wárah

Allow, to, prekhodal, (root), pregd

Allowance, májib (muwájib)

Alone, yawáze; zán lah

Also hum

Always, mùdám; hameshah; tol

And ao

Angry. khapah; pah qahar

Animal zanáwar

Answer zawáb

Appear, to, khkáredal

Apple manrah

Apricot zardálú

Appoint, to, moqararawul

Arise, to (get up) pásedal; portah kedal

Arm (body) lás

Arms (weopon) waslah

Army, lakhkar; fauz

Arrangement, bandúbast; sámán

Arrive, to, rasedal

Artillery, top khánah

Artillery (field) medáni top khánah

Artillery (horse) da asúno top khánah

Artillery (garrison) da qlá top khánah; dranah top khánah

Artillery (mountain) da ghrúno top khánah

Ascend, to, khatal (root) khej

Ask, to, pukhtanah kawul; pukhtal

Asleep uduh

At, pah ke

At all, bekhi; bilkul; hado

Attack, hamlah; chápah

Attack, to, hamlah kawul; chápah wahal

Autumn manai

Awaken, to, wikhawul

B.

Bachelor zalmai; lawand

Back, (the) shá

Back (adv) bertah; pastanah

Bad, nákárah; kharáp

Bag (gunny) bojá-i; borá-i

Bag (nose) tobrah

Bag (money) hamyáná-i

Baggage asbáb; sámán; bárbar-dári

Baker, batyárai; nánwá-i

Band (men) tolai; dalah

Band (play) bájah

Bank ghárah

Banker, khazánchi; saráf

Barbar ná-i

Bark, to, ghapal

Bar kará-i

Barley (pl.) orbushe

Barren (land) sbárah

Barrel (gun) shpelá-i

Basket tokrá-i

Bathe, to, lámbal, (casual) lam-bawul

Battle jang

Beyonet sangin

Be, to, become, kedal, root, "keg"; or shwal, root, "sh"

Bear melú

Beard girah

Beat, to, strike, to, wahal

Beat, to, music, ghagawul

Beautiful, kháistah; khkolai

Because, zakah chih; zakah

Bed kat

Before, place, mukh ke

Before, time, pakhwá; wránde; awal

Beggar faqir

Begin, to, shoru kawul; lás pore kawul

Behind, pah shá; wrasto

Believe, to, yaqin kawul

Belt, waist, kamarband; petá-i

Besides this, belah de nah; má sewá lah de nah

Bet, to, shart taral; shart lagawul

Betrothal kuzhdan

Betrothed youth, changhol

Belrothed girl, changhalah

Between, pah ke; pah meanz ke

Big loe

Bird márghuh

Bird, small. marghá-i

Bite, to, chichal

Bitter trikh

Black tor

Blanket, sharā-i; kamal

Blind, rúnd; mázúrah

Blaze, to, lambah kawuh

Blood, wine, winah, sing,

Boat berá-i

Boat, small, kishtá-i

Boat pulled by rope, da tanáo birá-i

Boatman mánrgai

Body, júsah; wajúd

Book kitáb

Borne, to be, pedá kedal

Border sarhad

Both dwárah

Boundry, had; bred; púlah

Box sandúq

Boy halak

Brave, túrzan; bahádar; zruhwar

Bravery túrzantob

Bread dodá-i

Breakfast nárai

Break, to, mátawul

Brick kbakhtah

Bride, náwe, pl. náwyáne

Bride groom, zalmai

Bridge púl

Bridge, of boats, da bero púl

Bridge, masonary, pokh púl

Bridge, rough, kacha púl

Bring, to, inan, ràwral, root, ráwar

Bring, to, ani, ráwastal, root, ráwal

Broad plan

Broken, to be, mátedel

Bucket, for drawing water, boqah

Bucket, horse, bàltá-i or báltai

Buffelo, cow, mekhah

Buffelo, bull, sandá

Buffoon naqli

Bugler, begalchi; toramchi

Building wadáni

Build, to, wadánawul; abádawul

Bullet gola-i

Bullseye, gulziyarai

Bull, stallion, sán

Bundle, clothes etc. pand, small, pandúkai

Bundle, wood etc. gaidai

Burden, bár; pand

Burglary kandar

Burn, to v. t. swazawul; sezal

Burn, to v. int. swazẹdal

Bush járah

Busy, náwúzgár, lagyá

Butcher qasáb

But, kho; wale; magar; lekin

Butt, nakhah; cháomári

Butt, gun, kundágh

Butter kuch

Buy, to, pah bayah akhistal, root, akhl

By chance, násápah; nághánah

By God, khudá-ego

C.

Cabbage gopi

Cage pinjrah

Calamity, balá; áfat

Calf, caw, skhai

Calf, buffaloe, katai

Call, to, balal

Camel aúkh

Camping ground, paráo

Campaign lám

Canal, walah, wáluh

Candidate aomedwár

Cane baint

Cane, to, pah baintúno wahal

Cannon topah

Cantonment cháwnrá-i

Cap, wearing, topá-i

Caravan qáfelah

Care, to take, paham kawul; khabardári kawul

Careless beparwá

Careful, khabardárah; watchful, or at alert, bedár

Carpet, qáleen, dará-i, woolen, lamsai

Carriage, cart, gádai

Carry, to, inan. wral root "yaos" or "wr"

Carry, to, anim. bival or botlal, root "boz" or ' biya"

Cartridge kàrtús

Cash rok m, rokah f. s.; naqad, naqdah f. s.

Cashier, saráf; khazánchi

Caste, qaum; asal; zát

Cat pisho f

Catch, to, niwal, root, "nis"

Cattle, dangar; mál; sárwi

Cause, sabab; wajah

Cavalry, regiment, risálah

Cavalryman, sor; swáruh; plu

Cave, smas; ghár

Cell, lock up, hawálát

Century, perá-i; sadá-i

Chaff bús

Chain zanzir

Chair kúrsá-i

Change, to, badalawul

Charcoal skáruh

Cheap arzán

Chief, khan; malak, mashar

Child, bachai; babay, másúm

Children, halakán jinaká-i; wáruh záguh

Cholera, wabá; hezah

Church giljah

City, khár, small, kháriyah

Clasp kará-i

Class darjah

Class, school, jamá-at

Clean, pák; sáf; pákizah

Cliff kamar

Climate ábu hawá

Climb, to, khatal; root "khej"

Close nizde

Cloud waryaz

Clue, darak; patah

Clump of trees, jangá-i; banr

Coat, cloak, khalqah

Cock chirg

Coffin, tábút

Cold, yakh; sor

Collect, to, tolawul; jamah kwul, yau záe kawul

Colour rang

Colour, to, rangawul

Colour, flag, jandah

Comb gamanz

Come, to, rátlal root "ráz" or "rásh",

Commanding officir, kamán afsar

Commander in chief, sepáh sálár; jangi lát

Companion, malgarai, mal

Company kampaná-i

Complaint, official, shikáyat, nálish

Complaint, private, gilah

Complainant, legal, mudda-i; mustaghis

Compound house, gholai

Congratulation, mubáraki; zerai

Congratulate, to v t. mubáraki warkawul v. int. mubárak kedal root "mubáraksh"

Conceal, to v. t. Patawul

Condition, state, hál, terms, shart

Conquer, to, fatah kawul; lánde kawul

Contract thekah

Contractor thekadár

Conversation, khabare atare

Convrse, to, khabare kawul

Convicted, sazáyabe; mujrim

Convoy badraqah

Cook, to, pakhawul

Cooked, to be, pakhedal, root, "pokhsh"

Cool, to yakhawul; sarawul

Corporal ná-ik

Corporal, lance, lais ná-ik

Corn ghalah

Corpse marai

Correct sahih

Cotton, uncleaned, pumbah

Cotton, cleaned, málúch

Council, tribal, jargah

Count, to, shmeral

Country mulk

Country, native, watan

Court, of king, darbár

Court, of justice, kachará-i

Court yard, gholai

Courtier, darbári, ahlekár

Cousin tarbúr

Credit, por; qaraz

Criple shal

Crop fasal

Cross, to. v. in. porewatal, root, "porewúz"

Cry, to v, t. jaral

Cultivate, to, karal

Cultivation, karwinoah; kar

Cultivator zamindár

Curds mástuh

Cure, to, illáj kawul

Cured, to be, illáj kedal

Curse, to, khere kawul

Curtain pardah

Custom, dastur; lár, rawáj

Cut, to, prekawul; ghosawul

D.

Dagger, pesh qozah

Daily, harah wraz; da wraze wraze

Dance, to, gadedal

Danger, yarah; khatarah; khaof

Dangerous khatarnák

Darkness tiyáruh

Date tárikh

Dead mur

Deaf kúnr

Debt qaraz

Debtor qarazdár

Decieve, to, ghlawul

Decide, to, feslah kawul

Deep jawar

Dear gráu

Delay, drang; deel

Descend, to v. int. kúzedal

Decendents aulád; záúzád

Descent, kuzedanah

Desert merah

Destroy, to v. t. wránawul; barbáda-
wul

Dew, parkhah

Die, to, mral; mar kedal

Different, biyal biyal, júdá júdá

Dig, to, kanastal; kanodal, root,
"kan"

Direction f, s. khwá; dadah; lore;
táraf, palau

Dirty, khiran

Disease, maraz; nájortiyá; ranz;
bimári

Dismiss, to, from service, nokará-i
nah estal

Dismount, to, kúzedal

District zilah; aláqah

Dispatch, legal; astawul

Desturb, to. tangawul

Ditch, moat, khandaq

Divide, to, weshal; brakhe kawul

Dome, gúmbat

Domestic, koranai

Door, war; darwázah

Dot takai

Double bragh

Doubtful shakman

Down, kùz; khkatah

Drain lakhtai

Dream khob

Dream, to, khob lidal

Drill, kawá id; parait

Drive, to, cart etc. chalawul

Drive away, to, sharal

Drop sáskaı

Drought sokrah

Drawn, to, dúbawul

Drawn, to be, dúbedal

Drum damámah; nghárah; doì

Drummer, dam; nghárchi

Drunkard sharábi

Dry, to wuchawul

Dried, to be, wuchedal

Dung, of horses, khashnruh

Dung, of cattle, súte

Dung, dried of cattle, ghushayán

Dung, of camel, sheep, goat etc.,
pache

Dust dúrah

Dust, to, sandal

Duty nokari

Dwell, to, aosedal, root, "aos"

E.

Early wakhti

Earn, to, gatal

Earth kháwrah

Earthen, da kháwre

Earthquake zaizalah

Easy asán

Eat, to, khwaral

Eclipse, to, tandar niwal

Edge, of house, banerah

Edge, of field, púlah

Effect asar

Elder, mashar; spingeerai

Empty tash; kháli

End, sar; akhir; intehá

Engage, to, nokarawul

Engaged lagyá

Enough, bas; káfi

Enter, to, nanawatal, root, nana-
wúz

Equal brábar

Escape, to, khlásedal; bachkedal

Especially khás

Estimate, to, andázah kawul; andázah lagawul

Every one, har yao

Evil badi

Examine, to imtehán akhistal

Examine to be, imtehán kedal

Examiner, imtehán wálah

Example misál, matal

Excessively be haddah; beshánah

Excuse, úzar; bahánah; hilah

Excuse, to ma-áfawul; bakhal

Executor jalád

Expect, to, da chá lár katal

Expense, khars; lagakht

Experience, tajrebah; azmaikht

Experience, to, **azmaikht kawul**
Experienced, **tajrebakár**
Explain, to, **pohawul, bayánawul**
Extract, to, **waistal, aistal, aubásal, root aubás**

F.

Face, **makh**
Fact, **ma-ámelah, wáqeah**
Factory, **kár khánah**
Fail, to, fail **kedal**
Fair, **melah, spin, white**
Fairy, **kháperai**
Faithful, **namak hálál, emándár, wafádár**
Faithless, **namak harám, be emánah, be wafá**
Fairy, **kháperai**
Fall, to, **prewatal. root, "prewúz"**
Fall down. to, **lwedal**
Family, **tabar,**
Family, lineage, **khánadán asal**
Family, high **khánawádah**
Famine, **qáhat**
Famous, **mashahúr**
Fan, **babozai**
Fan, to, **babozai wahal**
Far, **larai**
Far, from a, lah **wráyah**
Farm labour, **charikár, dihqán**
Farmer, **zamidár**
Farrier, **nálband**
Fast, ad, **garandai, jalt, tez**
Fasten, to v. t. **taral**
Fasting, **nahár**
Fat, ad. **ghat, pairr, sorab**
Fate, **qismat**
Fatigue party, **halah gúlah**
Fault, **qasúr, gúnáh, aib, noqsáh**
Fear, **werah**
Fear, to, **weredal, animals, taredal**
Feast, **doda-i, melmastiyá**
Festival, small, **warúkai akhtar**
Festival, big, loe **akhtar**

Fetters, **zolanai**
Feud, **patnah badi**
Field, **patai**
Fight, **jang, jagarah**
Fighter, **jangi**
Fill to, **dakawul**
Find, to, **mandal, root, mum**
Finish, to, v. t. **khlásawul**
Finish to v. int. **khlásedal**
Fire, **aor**
Fire, a shot of gun, **daz**
Fire, to, shoot with a gun etc., **wishtal, root, wul**
Fire, to, a gun, **topak khlásawul**
First, **awal, wrúmbai**
First **súk**
Fit, to, v. t. **biál árawul**
Fit, to, v. int. **brábaredal**
Fix, to v. t. **lagawul**
Flag, **jandah**
Flame, **lambah**
Flat, level; **hawár**
Flee, to, **takhtedal, root, "takht"**
Floor, **zmakah**
Flooring, **farsh**
Flow, to, **bahedal**
Fly, to **alwátel, root, 'alúz"**
Foam, **zag**
Fog, **dúnd**
Fond, ad, **shoqi, shoqin**
Forbid, to, **mana kawul**
Force, **zor**
Forcibly, **pah zor**
Forefathers, **plár nikúna**
Foreign, **pradai**
Foreigner, **bahránai**
Forget, to, be **rawul**
Forgive, to, **bakhal**
Former, **pakhwánai**
Formerly, **pakhwá, wrúmbai**
Fortnight, **dwah jume, dwah hafte**
Foundation, of building, **radah**
Fountain, **chinah**
Free, let out, **khlás, azád**
Free, at liesure, **wúzgár**

Free, gratis, weryá
Freeze, to kangal kedal
Fresh, tázah
Friday, júmah
Friend, ashná, yár, beloved
Friendship, ashná-i, yári
Frighten, to, yarawul, tarawul
Frightened, to be, yaredal, tare-
dal
Future pas tah, pas lah de

G

Gain, to, v. t. gatal
Gamble, to v. t jowári kawul
Gambling, juwári
Gambler, jowárgar
Game, lobah, sport, khkár
Gate, loeyah darwázah, pátak
Geld, to, khasi kawul
Generation, perá i, sadá-i
Generous, sakhi, sakháwati
Gentleman, khánawádah, khánkhel,
safaid-poshai, ashráf, aseel
Gift, manakhtah, shúkránah, nazar
Girth, tang
Glad, khushál, khushálah
Glass, khikhah
Glass, looking, á-inah
Glitter, to, zaledal
Go, to, tlal, root, "z" or "lársh"
Goad, chúkah
God, khudá-e
Gold, coin, ashrafá-i
Good khuh
Goodness, neki
Goods and chattels, kadah
Govern, to, hokam kawul
Governor, hákim
Grandson, nwasai
Grateful, ehsánmand, shokar
gúzára
Gratis, weriyá, khairát
Graze, to, v. t. sarawul
Graze, to, v. t. int. saral, saredal
Grazing ground, warsho

Greasy, ghwar
Greedy heras-nák
Greet, to, jortázah kawul
Grief, gham, armán
Grind, to, aorawul
Ground, zmakah
Grow, to, v. int. loedal, pedá
kedal
Grow, to, v. t., crops, karal
Grow, to, v. in., to vegetate,
túkedal
Guest, melmah, melmanah, f.
Guest house, hujrah
Guilty, mojrim, gúnáhgár
Gun, rifle, topak
Gun, cannon, topah
Gutter, náwah, parnálah

H.

Habit, ádit, khúi
Half, nim
Hall, dálán
Halt, to, derah lagawul, maqám
kawul
Hand over, to, spáral, hawálah
kawul
Handmill, mechan
Hanged, to, v. t. zwarandawul,
awezándawul
Hang, to, death, phánsi kawul
Hang, to, be, death, phánsi kedal
Happen, to, v. in. pekhedal, kedal
Happy, khushál
Hard, klak, sakht
Harm, ziyán, noqsán
Hate, to, járawul
Have, to, laral
Headlong, sar da lánde, par makh
Health, tandrasti, sihhal
Heap, top, derai, ambár
Hear, to, awredal, root, "awr"
Hearth, stove, ngharai
Heavy, drúnd, dranah, f.
Heaven, janat
Hedge, shpol

Hell. dozakh

Help, to v. t. komak or, madat, kawul

Helpless, mohtáza, láchára

Hesitates. to, makhke wrasto kawul

Hidden, pat, panáh

Hide, to, patawul

Hill, ghar

Hilly. gharsanai, da ghruh

Hillock, ghúndá-i

Hinge, door, chúr

Hit, to, wishtal, root, "wul"

Hold, to, niwal, root, "nis"

Hold, to, fast, tingawul

Honest, emándár, amánatgar

Honesty, rásti

Honey, gabeen, shát

Honour, izzat

Honourable, izzatdára, izzatnák

Hope umed

Hopeful, umedwár

Hopeless, ná umeda

Hospitility, melmastiyá

Host, korbanah

Hot, tod, garm

Hour gentah

House, kor, karah, inflected

Hunt, to, khkár kawul

Hunter, khkári

Hurt. to, khúgawul

Hut, jùngarah

I.

Ice, snow, wáwrah

If, kah

Ignorance, nápohi

Ignorant, núpoha, jáhil, ami

Ill nájora

Illness, nájortiyá, ranz, bimári maraz

Illnature, bad khúi

Illtreat, to, bad kawul

Immediately, samdasti, yau dam

Important, zarúri

Imprison, to, qaidawul, bandi kawul

Imprisonment, qaid, band

Incite, to, lamsawul

Income, paidáwár, ámdani

Increase, to, ziyátawul

Incumbent, faraz, lázim

India, Hindustán

Indian, hinkai

Indus, abásind

Infant, máshúm

Influence, barakat, makh

Inform, to khabrawul

Informed, to be, khabredal

Informer, mokhbir

Inhabitants, aosedúnki

Injure, to, ziyáe, or zarar, rasawul

Ink, siyáhi

Insipid, pikah

Insist upon, to, tákid kawul

Instead of, pah zá-e, pah badal ke

Intelligence, hokhiyártiyá

Intend, to, v. t. niyat, or qasd, kawul

Intention, niyat

Intentionally, lah qasda nah

Interpret, to v. t. tarjumah kawul

Interpretor, n. tarjumah kawúnkai

Interruption, khalal

Introduce, to, makhá makh kawul, baladawul

Intrust, to, spáral, hawálah kawul

In vain abas

Invent, to v. t. rawánawul, jorawul

Island, jazirah, belah, tápù

Issue, to, v. t. jári kawul, warkawul

Itch, to, v. int. khárakhtedal

J.

Jealous, n. qasdjan, bughzi

Jest, n. toqah

Jester, n. toqmár
Jewel, n. gohar
Jewels, ornaments, káli
Jolt, n. dikah. jútah
Journal, roznámchah
Journey, mazal, safar
Joy, n. khusháli, khádi
Judge, to, v t. insáf kawul
Jump, to, dangal, top wahal

K.

Keen, on, shoqin
Keep, to. v. t. sátal
Key, n. kúnji
Kill, to, v. t. wajal, root, "wajn"
King, n. Báchá
Kingdom, báchá-i
Kiss, to. v. t. khkolawul
Knock down, to, anim, parzawul
Knock down, to, house etc., narawul
Knot, n. ghotah
Knot to, v. t ghotah kawul, ghatah achawul
Know. to v. t. understand, pohedal root, "poheg"
Know, to, v. t., recognize, pejandal, root, "pejan"
Known, málúm
Known, to be, v int. malúmedal
Knowledge, n. elam

L.

Laborious, n. khwárikakh
Labour. work. mihnat, mazdúri
Labourer, mazdúr
Ladder, andarpáyah, pársang
Land, zmakah
Lane, kúsah
Language, jabah, or, zhabah
Last, wrostai
Late, náwakhta
Laugh, to, v. int. khándal

Lead, to, v. t. botlal, root, "boz" bival, root, "biyá"
Leak, to, v. int. sasedal
Leap, to, v. int. dangal, topúnah wahal
Learn, to, v t. zdah kawul
Learned man, álim
Lease, n. ejárah
Leather, n. sarman
Leave. of absence, chúti, chútá-i
Left, gas, kinr
Liesure, wúzgártiyá
Lend, to, qarz, or por warkawul
Less, kam, lag
Lest, conj, hase nah chih
Let, to, v. t. prekhodal, root, "pregd"
Let, to, on hire, pah kra-i warkawul
Leval a, hawár
Lick, to v. t. satal
Life, body, zán
Life, time. jwand, jwandún
Lift, to, úchatawul, portakawul
Light, n not dark, ronrá, rokhná-i
Light, a, not heavy, spak
Light, to, balawul
Lightning, tandar, braqá, brekhrá
Liked, pleasant, khwakh
Lisp. to, v. int jabah nkhatal
List, fahrist
Listen, to, v. int. awredal, root, "awr"
Little, opposite to big. warúkai
Little. opposite to much, lag, lagkúti
Live, to, v. int. dwell, aosedal, root, "aos"
Live on, to, v. t. on pay etc. gúzrán kawul
Living, livelihood, guzárah
Load bár
Load, half, andai
Load, to be carried on person, pand

Load, to, bárawul, legdawul
Loadstone, áhin-robá
Loan, qaraz, por
Lock jandrah, qulf
Lock up, to, jandrah wahal
Lock up, cell, hawálát
Locusts, mlakhán
Log, wood, stah, ghúnd
Logs, cut down in heep, hair
Lonely, yawázai
Lonely, place, khúshai
Look, to v. t katal root, "gor"
Look for, to, persons, lár katal
Look for, to, things, latawul
Look, n. aspect, shikal, serah
Loose, to, animals, pránastal, root, "pránaz"
Loose, to be, klásedal, pránastai kedal
Lose, to, wrokawul
Lost, to be, wrokedal
Lost, wrok
Loss, ziyán, noqsán
Lots, to, cast, hisk, or pachah, achawul
Love, to, minah kawul
Love, to fall in, mayan kedal
Lover, yár, mayan, áshiq
Low, khkatah, lánde, kúz
Loyal, namak-halál
Luck bakht
Lucky, bakhtawar
Luggage samán, asbáb

M.

Mad, lewanai
Madam, khánah, bibi, sáhibah
Made, to be, v. i., joredal, root, "joreg"
Magic, jádú, kode
Magician, jádúgar
Maid, peghlah
Make, to, v. t., jorawul, root, "jorkw"
M'aker, n., jorawúnkai

Male, nar
Malice, kinah, qasad
Manage, to, v. t., sambálawul
Manager, n , ekhtiyármand
Manliness, manly, saritob
Map, naqshah
Marsh, bokhtanah, jabah
Master, owner, sakhtan, ná-ik, málik kbáwand
Master, teacher, ustáz, or, ustád
Mat, n,. púzai, big, púwar
Match, n., tilai
Mate. madatgár, sha·ikwál, malgarai
Material, building, etc., masá-lah, malbah
Matter, affair, n , khabarah, ma-ámelah
Maund, n , 80 ibs. mun
Meaning, meau, máne matlab
Meaningless. be-máne
Measure. n kach, mech, pemánah
Measure to, v. t., kach, or mech, kawul
Medial, meanzanai. miyánah
Meet, to, v. t., visit, lidal, root, "win"
Meet. to v. i., to, come across, pekhedal
Meet, to together, you zá-e kedal
Meating. jalsah, majlas
Memorial, n., yádgár
Milt. to, v. i., weele kedal
Mention to, v. t , zikar kawul, yádawul
Mercy, raham, zruh swai
Method, lár, tariqah, chal
Middle. meanz
Mill, hand, n. mechan
Mill, water, n. jrandah
Miller, n. jrandagarai
Misfortune, n., bad nasibi, kam-bakhti
Mistake n., ghalati, khatá-i
Mistake a road, to, lar khatá kawul, lár ghalatawul

Mistaken, to be, to miss, khatá
  kedal
Mix, to, v. t., gadawul, yao záe
  kawul
Modern a, aosanai
Modest, hayá-nák, ghairati, sha-
  ramnák
Money, rúpái
Month, Miyásht
Moon, n., spogmá i
Mound, n , derá-i, ghunda-i
Mount, to, v. t. on horse etc.,
  swaredal
Mount, to, v. t. ascend, khatal
Mountain, n. ghar
Mountaineer, gharsanai, kohistánai.
Mourn, to, v. t., wir, or úzar,
  kawul
Mouthful, bread, nwará-i
Mouthful, water, gút
Move, to v. t., khwazawul
Move, to, v. i, khwazedal
Mutiny, balwah, ghadar, pasát
Mutineer, pasáti, balwahgar

N.

Naked, a, barband, laghar
Name, n., núm
Name, to, v. t, núm kekhodal
Nasty, a, nápák, múrdár, paleed
Necessary, a, zarúr, lázim
Needful, a, mútáza, hájatmand
Needy, ad, mutáj, mútáz
Neglect, n., ghaflat, beparwá-i
  kawul
Neglectful, a, gháfil, beparwá
Negro, n., habshi
Neighbour, n., gwándi
Nervous, a. wárkhatá, or zorawar
News, n., khabar
Newspaper, n., ikhbár, da khaba-
  rúno kághaz
Nice, a, fine. der khuh
Nice, a, delicious, da maze, khwand
  nák
Night, n. f. s. shpah

Noble, of high family, khána-
  wádah
Noise, n, awáz, shor, zwag, ghag
Nonsense, n., abas, be máne, púch
Note, chit, n., chita-i, parchah,
  kághaz
Notice, n., ishtehár, khabar, notas
Nourish, to, v. t., pálal, palanah
  kawul
Nourish, to, v. i,. pá-edal
Nourisher, n., sátúnkai, pálúnkai
Nourishment, n. pálanah, sátanah
Number, figure, hindse, shmár
Number, to, v. t. shmeral, shmáral
Numerous, a, der, ziyát, balá,
  makhlúq

O.

Oath, to take, v. t., qasam, or sou-
  gand khwaral
Oath, to give, v. c , qasam, or
  sougand, warkawul
Obey, to, v. t., hokam manal,
  manal
Object, to, v. t., uzar, hujat,
  kawul
Oblige, to, by force, be wasa, or
  pah zor kawul
Oblige. to, by favours, ehsánmand
  kawul
Obtain, to, v. t. básilawul, bivá
  múndal
Occupied, busy, lagyá, mashghúl
Occupy, to, v. t., dwell, aosedal,
  r, "aos"
Occur v. i., pekhedal, kedal
Offer, to, a present, peshkash
  warkawul
Office, dafter
Official, sarkári, daftari
Officiating, pah za-e, or maqám,
  pah badal ke
Often, aksar, der zalah, der wárah
Once' yauzal, yau wár, yao gúzár
Only, tash, kháli, faqat

Oper, to, v. t., pránastal, r, "prá-naz"

Open, to, v. t.; door etc. lare kawul

Opinion, n., khiyál, fikar, gúmán

Opportunity moqah

Opposite a, makhà makh

Oppression, zolam, zor ziyátai

Oppression, medically, jaráhi kawul

Oral, zobáni, wayená

Order, n., hokam

Original, a, asli

Orphan, n, yateen

Ought, ad, khá-i. p kár, or muná sib, di

Outbreak, pasát, balwah, maraz, sickness

Outlaw, farári, mafrúr, yághi

Outpost, n., sauká-i

Outrage, n., zolam, ziyátai

Outside, out, bahar

Outwardly, ad. záherah

Over come, to, v. t., lánde kawul, mátah warkawul

Overflow, to, v. i., láhú kedal

Owe, to, v. i., qarazdár kedal

Own, a, khpal

Owner, sakhtan, kháwand, málik

P

Pace, step, qadam, gám, long step

Pace, to, to take a step, qadam akhishtal

Page, n., of book, or leaf, pánrah

Pain, n., dard, khúg

Painstaking man, khwári kakh sarai

Paint, to, v. t., dye, rangawul, rang kawul

Painter, n., rangsáz, dobi

Pale, yellow ziyar

Part, share, brakhah, hisah

Partner, sharikwál, hisah-dár

Pass, to, v. i., road, teredal, r, "tersh" or "tereg"

Pass, to, v t., terawul. r. "terkar"

Pass, to, v. i., in exam., pás-kedal

Passenger, n., músáfir, ráh-rawai, wayfarer

Passport n., ráh-dári, parwánah

Past, in time tair, tairrshawai

Paste, letá-i

Patience, n., sabar

Patient, not hasty, sabar-nák

Patient sick, ranzúr, mariz, nájorah

Pattern, n., namúnah

Pay, tankhwá, talab, májib

Perfect, complete, kámil, púrah

Perform to, v. t., púrah, or adà, kawul

Perhaps, ad, gunde, sháyad

Period, n, long time, múdah

Perish, to v. i., faná kedal

Permanent, a, pokh, mustaqil

Permission, n ijáz h, izan

Permit, to, v. t., ejázah, or ezan kawul

Personally, ad pukhpalah pah khpal zán

Philosopher, n., hakim

Phrase. n, kalimah, fiqrah, júmlah

Picture, n., serah

Piece, n., túkrah

Pierce, to, v. t., chúkah kawul, tùmbal

Pierce, to, v. i. chúkah kedal

Pillar, n., stan, feel páyah

Pit, n, doghal kandah

Pitch, to, v. t., tents etc., udrawul, lagawul, lakawul

Place, n.. zá-e, maqám

Plain n, medán dág

Plan, scheme, chal, band, tadbir

Platform, mound, chauntrah dùnkáchah

Play, to, v. t, lobe kawul

Play, to, v. t., music, ghagawul

Play, to, v. t., gambling, jowári kawul

Pleasant, a, khwakh

Plantiful, der, ziyát, makhlúq

Pock marks face, tape tape makh

Poem, n., sandarah, ghazal chárbetah

Poet, n., shá-ir

Poetry, n., sh-ir, ghazal, betúnah

Point, n., of weapon, súkah

Poor, n., khwár, gharib ájiz

Population n. abádi, wadáni

Populous, a, wadán, abád

Postpone, to v. t. mu-atalawul

Pour, to, v. t., achawul, r, "achaw"

Pour, to. v. t., shed, toyawul

Poverty n., ki wári, gharibi, tangsyá

Powerful, a, zorawar qawi takrah, mazbút

Practice, to, v t. mashq kawul

Praise, to, v. t., stáyal, sifat kawul

Precaution, n., ehtiyát, paham

Precede, to. v. t. wrande, or makhke, tlal

Precious, baish qimat, baish bahá

Prepare, to, v. t., tayárawul, v. i. tayáredal

Presence, n., házari, maujúdwálai

Present, a házir, maujúd

Present, n., a gift, peshkash

Press, to, v. t. zor kawul, or, zor warkawul

Press, n., printing cháp khánah

Pretence, n,, excuse, úzar, bhánah

Present, to, v. t. stop, manah kawul

Prick, to, v. i. pierce, chúkakedal

Pride n. kabar, gharúr

Prince, n., sháhzadah

Princess, n., gháhzádgá-i

Print, to, v. t., chápawul

Private, a, mámúli, khpal

Prize, reward, enám

Probably, gúnre, or, gúnde, sháyed

Proclaim, to, v. t., naqárah wahal damámah garzawul

Product, paidáwár, ámdan, básil

Progress, to, make v. t. taraçi, or zivátai, kawul

Promise, n,, lauz, wádah, eqrár

Promise, to, lauz kawul, zhabah kawul, eqrár kawul, wádah kawul

Promotion, n., taraqi

Promote, to, v. t., taraqi kawul, or v. i., taraqi kedal

Proper, a; khuh, sahih, khá-i, báeduh di, múnásib di, pakár di

Properly ad, pah khuh shám or, rang

Property, estate, mál

Propose, to, v. t, band taral, saláh kawul

Proposal, n., band, maslahat, tadbir

Prosperity, n., bakht, eqbál, barakat

Protection, n., baсháu, panáb, amán

Protect, to, v. t. bach kawul, v. i., bach kedal

Proud, n- kabarjan maghrúra

Proverb, n, matal

Province, n. súbah, aláquh, parganah, tapah

Public, a, ám khalq, aúlas, álam

Pull, to, v. t,, rákhkal, r, "rákág"

Pump, water, n., bambah

Punctual, n., in time, pah wakht

Punctual, n,, regular, da qá-ede, dastúri

Purpose, matlab gharaz. modda-á, kár

Push, to. v. t., telwahal, dikal

Put, to, place, v. t., kekhodal, ekhodal, gdal, roots. "kegd," or, "gd"

Put, to, v. t., apply on, lagawul, pore kawul

Q.

Quagmire, n., bokhtanah, lahah

Quality, n., greatness, sifat, johar, khásiyat

Quantity, n., andázah, shai

Quarrel, n., dispute, jagrah

Quarrel, to, v. t., jagrah kawul

Quarter, ¼, saloramah

Quarter, of a village, kandai, mahlat

Quarterly, 3 months seh máhi

Queen. n., malikah, bádsháhah

Question, n., sawál, pukhtanah

Question, to, v. t, sawál kawul

Quick a, garandai, jalt, chábak, tez

Quickly ad, zarzar, garandai

R.

Rag, n., a torn piece of cloth, chirrah

Raise, to. v. t., aúchatawul, porta-kawul khejáwul

Raise, to, v. i., khatal, porta kedal, aúchatedal

Rampart, n., panáhi, chárdewári

Reach, to, v. i', rasedal, root, "ras"

Ready, to, v t, lwastal, root, "lwal"

Ready, tayár

Real, a, asli

Really, n., pah asal ke, pah rikh-tiyá

Rear behind, pah shá, wrosto, dúmbál, pastanah

Reason, n., sabab, wajah

Recent, a aosanai

Reception, entertainment, receive, makhe lah tlal

Receive, to, recover, wasúlawul

Recommend, to, v. t. safárakht kawul

Reconcile, to, v. t., pukhlá kawul

Reduce, to, v. i., kamawul, máta-wul

Refuse, to, v. t., disobey. nah manal, enkár kawul, múnkare-dal

Regret, n., armán, afsos

Regret, to, v t., armán, kawul, khpemánedal, v. i.

Regular, a bá-qá-ede, da láre

Relay, to, v t, trust, báwar kawul

Relay, to, v. t., on God, tawkal, or ásrah, kawul

Remain, to, v. i., pátekedal

Remander. n. báqi, páte

Remember to, recollect, yádawul

Remember, to, bear in mind, yád laral

Remind, to, v. t, yádawul or yád-kawul

Remove, to v. t., lare-kawul

Repair, to, v. t., muramat-kawul, jorawul

Reply, to, v t.. zawàb-warkawul

Reputation, n., khuh, núm, masha-húri

Require, to, v. t., ghokhtal, r, "ghwár"

Required, to be, v. i., pakáredal, ghokht lai kedal

Requisition, n., pakár, zarúri, hajat

Respectable, n, izzat dár, motabar

Responsible. n., zemawár, zá-e

Rest, n., báqi, páte

Rest, to, v.i., damah khwaral, arám káwul

Result, n., natijah, akhir

Return, to, come back bertah, or, pastanah rátlal, ágarzedal, rájár watal,

Review, n.. nandárah, tamáshah

Reward, n, inám

Rich, man mor, daulat mand, máldár, dúnyádár

Ride, to, v. i., swaredal, r, "sorsh"

Ride, to, v. t, swarli kawul

Rider, n., sor, swarah f.

Ridge, a steep band ot river etc., kamar

Ridge, n., a summit, ghákhai

Right, correct, sahih, brábar

Right, true, rikhtiyá

Rise, to, v. t., khatal. r, "khej"

Robe of honour, n , khilat

Rock, n., gat, tigah

Roll. to, v. i., nghakhtal, r! "nghár"

Rope, a large cord, biyástah

Rope, a small cord, parai

Rope, a string mazai

Rough, a, zig ziga

Rule, regulation, qá edah qánún, áeen

Rule to, v. t hokam kawul

Ruler, n., hákim

Running, n., dau, mandah

Run, to, v. t. zghaledal r, "zghal"

Run away to, flee, takhtedal, r, "takht"

Run to, doubl, mandah, or dau, wahal

Run on, to, carry on work etc., chalawul. r, "chalaw"

Run away with to, zghalawul, takhtawul, kidnap

Run, through, to, dash against, takarah khwaral or wahal

Run on, to, v. i., going on work etc., chaledal, r, "chaleg"

Running. a, jári, rawán

Rust, n., zang, khirai

S.

Sad, a, ghamjan, zahir

Safe, a, salámat, sahih salámat, rogh jor

Safety, n., salámati

Sample, n., nakhah, namúnah

Sand, n., shagah

Sandy, a shaglorai

Satisfection, n. tasali, zruh jami

Satisfy, to, v i., rázi kedal, khosháledal, khwá yakhedal

Satisfy, to, v. t, rázi kawul, khoshálawul, zruh yakhawul

Save, to, v. t., bach kawul, sátal

Say, to, v. t., wayal, khabare kawul, converse

Scar. n., dágh, nakhah

Scarce, a, khál khál, kam, lag

Scarcity, n., pah sakhta-i, kamái, kam, lag

Scratch, to, v t., garawul

Search, to, v. t., latawul, darak lagawul

Secret, a, pat, panáh, da parde

Seem, to be, v. i., khkáredal, pah nazar rátlal, málúmedal

Select, to, v. t., anrawul, khwakhawul

Selfish, a, gharazi, matlabi

Send to, v. t., astawul legal

Send for, to, rághokhtal, r, "rághwár"

Send for, to, call, balal, r, 'bal'

Separate, a, júdá, biyal

Separate, to, v. t., júdá kawul, biyalawul

Separate, to, v. i, biyaledal, júdá kedal

Separation, n., biltún, júdá-i

Separately. ad, biyal biyal, júdá júdá

Set out, to, start off, rawánedal, r, "rawáneg"

Set free, to, khlásawul, azádawul

Several, a, der, aksar, chandá

Severe, a, sakht, mazbút, klak, pokh

Shade, n, sorai

Shake, to, v. t., khwazawul, v. i., khwazedal

Shame. n., sharam, hayá, ghairat

Shame, to, v. i., sharmedal

Skame. to, v. casual, sharmawul

Shameful. a, sharamnák, hayánák, ghairti, or, ghairatnák

Shameless a, besharma, behayá, be ghairata

Shape n., shikal, súrat, serah

Share, n., brakhah, hisah

Shout, to, náre wahal, awáz káwul, chagha waistal.

Show, to, v. t., khayal, r, "kháy"

Shut, to, v. t., pore kawul, banda-wul

Sigh, to, v. t., aswelai kawul

Silent, a, ghalai, qalár, chup

Silly, n., sádah, be-aqla

Since, ad, ráse

Sit, to, v. i., kenástal r, "ken"

Slave, n., mra-ai, winzah, girl

Sleep, n., khob

Sleep, to, v i úduh kedal, v. t., khob kawul

Sleepy, to be, v. i., khob rá, dar, war tlal

Slow, a wro

Slowly ad, wro wro

Smart a, strong, mazbút, tandrast,

Smart, a, active, chálák

Smile to, v. i., múskai kedal

Smoke n., lúgai

Smoke to, tobacco tamáků skal

Smoke, to, a pipe, chilam skal

Sneeze, to, engai kawul

Society, n., majlas, dalah

Some, ad, ziue, báze, sah

Song, n, sandarah, sandare, pl.

Soon, ad, zar jalt

Sore, a, hurt khúg

Sore back khúga shá, lagedale shá

Sorrow, n., gham, armán

Sorrowful, a ghamjan, khapah, armáni

Soul, breath, n., sáh, arwáh

Soul. of shoes, talai, palm of hand

Sp n n., a measure, baisht thumb to the end of the bettle finger

Spare, a, terai, ziyáte

Spare, to, v. t., ziyáti kawul

Speak, to, v. t., khabare kawul

Special a, khás

Specimen, n., nawúnah, misál

Spectacle, nandárah, tamáshah

Spectacles, for eyes, chishme

Spectators, n., da tamáshe khalq, tamáshgar

Split, to, v. t., chawul, v. 1., cháwdal, r, "chaw"

Spoil, to, v. t., wránawul. kharápawul

Spoiled, to be, wránelal, kharápedal

Spot, n, dágh, nakbah

Spot, n., place, moqah. zá-e

Spr in. to, v. i., iá ked al, táo k w ral

Stand, to, v. i., udredal, r, 'udreg"

Stand fast. in fighting etc., tinge-dal

State, condition, hál

Stay, to, v. i., pátekedal, he áredal

Step, pace qadam, long race, gám

Stick, to, v. i., nkhatal, r, "nkhal"

Stick to, v. t. nkhalawul, r, "nkha-law"

Strange, a, foreiguer, pradai, báhránai

Stretch, to, v. t., úgdawul, ghazawul

Stretch, to, v. i., úgdedal, ghazedal

Stumble, to, tindak khwaral, or, wahal

Succeed, to, matlab tah rasedal

Successful, a maqsúdmand, bare-nák

Successor, n., qá emúqám

Suddenly, ad, nasápah nágabánah

Suffer, to. bear zghamal

Sufficient bas der, káfi

Sure, n., belief báwar yaqin

Suspend to, hang zwarandawul, awezándawul

Suspend, to, to cause to cease, mu-atelawul

Sweat n., khwale, v. i., khwale kedal

Sweet, a, khog

Swing, n., tál, v. t., zángal, v. c., zangawul

Sympathy, n., zruh swai, khúg

T.

Take, to, or buy, akhistal r, "akhl"
Take away, to, anim, botlal, r, "boz"
Tak away, inanim, wral, r, "yaos" or, "wr"
Tale, n., story, qisah, qisà-i
Talk, to, v t., khabare kawul
Tear to, v. t., shlawul. sire kawul v. i shledal, sirekedal
Tears, n.. aukhke
Tease, to, oppress tangawul
Tell, to, say, wayal. r, "way"
Temper, n.. habit. khúi, adat, ta-bah
Test, v t., azm yal, azmekht kawul
Therefore. ad, zakah chib, zakah
Thing, n.. shai, siz
Thirst n., tandah
Thirsty, a, tagai
Thirsty, to feel, tagai kedal
Thought, n., gúnán, fikar, khiyál aq il
Throw away, to, ghorzawul
Throw, to, liquid, toeyawul, r, "toeyaw"
Tittle, n., khitáb, neknámi
Too, adv. hum, ziyát, der
Touch, to, v t, lás warwral
Tremple, to, v. t., latárawul, ghoblawul, chikhrekawul
Tremble, to, v. i, ragedal, regdedal, larzedal
Trial, n, azmekhat, emehán, moqadema'u
Trick, n., chal, tagi
Trouble, n., rubar, sakhti
True a, not false, rikhtiyá, rishtenai
Truly, adv. pah rikhtiyá sarah, pah rástá-i
Trust, n, itbár, yaqin
Trustee, n., amánatgar, zimawár
Truth, n, rikhtiyá
Truthful, a rikhtinai, rástbáz
Try, to, v. t., Sá-i kawul, koshish kawul

Turn, to, v. i., garzawul, v. i., garzedal
Turn back, to, járwatal, r, "járwúz"
Turn out, to, drive out, sharal, r, "shar"
Twin, a pair jorah, bragh
Twirl, to, v. t., garzawul, táwaul
Twist to, v. i., táwedal, garzedal

U.

Udder, breast, tai, ti, pl.
Unaware, ná-khabarah
Upset, to, v.t., arawul, v. i, awredal
Urgent, a, zarúri, pakár
Use, to, v t, estemálawul
Useful, a, pakár, súdman, da fáede
Useless, a, ná-kára, be súda, be fáede
Usually, adv, aksar, múdám

V.

Varrious, a, rangá rang, qisma ajsm
Violence, n., zor ziyátai, zolam
Vioce, n., awáz, ghag, zwag shor
Virtue, n, neki, khuh
Visit, to, lidal. r, "win"

W.

Wait, to, v. i., hesáredal, pátekedal
Wait for, to, persons, da chá lár katal, r, "gor"
Wake, to. v. i., wikhedal
Waken, to, v. t., wikhawul
Want, to, v. t., ghokhtal, r, "ghwár"
Warn, to, v. t., khabrawul v. i., khabredal
Wealth, n., daulat, mál
Wealthy, a, rich, mor, daulatmand
Weep, to, v. t., jaral

Weeping, n., jará
Wick, n., lamp, bátá-i
Wicked, a, bad ná-kárah
Widow, n., kúndah
Widower, n. kúnd
Willing, a. rázi, khwakh, tayár
Wisdom, n., aqal, hokhiyártiyá, illam, pohah
Wise, a, hokbiyár, poha or po he
With, prep, sarah
Without, prep. be lah, baghair, má sewá
Wonder, to, heránedal
Wonderful, a, ajeeb h
World, n., dúnyá, jihán, álam

X.

Xerotes, da badan khúshki

Y.

Yard, n., gaz
Yawn, to, v. t., aswelai, mai kawul
Yawn, n. aswelai, ag
Year, n., kál, yearly kál pai.
Yeast, n., khambirah
Yok, n., jagh
Yoke fellow, n., hamzolai
Yond r, a, warhistah haghah khwá
You g, a warúkai
Younges , n , der warúkai
Youth. n., zwán, zalmai

Z.

Zeallous, a. shoqi sargaram
Zebra, n., gozekhar
Zinc, n., jast

THE END.

Empire Press, Nowshera.